THE INTERFERENCE THEORY OF GOVERNMENT.

BY

CHARLES ASTOR BRISTED,

MEMBER OF THE EXECUTIVE COMMITTEE, AND EX-CORRESPONDING SECRETARY OF THE AMERICAN FREE-TRADE LEAGUE.

"The League protests against the 'paternal' interference of Government with private pursuits, being convinced that the less Government is felt and seen, the better for all concerned."—*Manifesto of the American Free-Trade League.*

NEW YORK:
LEYPOLDT & HOLT,
1867.

LITTLE, RENNIE & CO.,
PRINTERS, STEREOTYPERS, AND ELECTROTYPERS,
430 BROOME STREET, N. Y.

TO

PROFESSOR ARTHUR LATHAM PERRY,

OF WILLIAMS COLLEGE,

WITH MUCH RESPECT

EOR HIS INTELLIGENCE AND INDEPENDENCE,

THIS BOOK IS DEDICATED.

CONTENTS.

CHAPTER I.

Causes of Interference.

CHAPTER II.

Errors of Interference.

CHAPTER III.

The Prohibition Stage of the Aquarian Movement.

THE INTERFERENCE THEORY OF GOVERNMENT.

CHAPTER I.

Causes of Interference.

The "policeman" theory of government.—Reaction against it.—Force *vs.* intellect.—Reaction in favor of strong government.—Louis Napoleon's success, and its effects on different countries.—The Mormons.—Our war.—Ignorance of and indifference to side issues.—The Puritan spirit the link between strength and interference.—The aquarian or so-called temperance movement.—French socialism.

MANY intelligent men have lately noticed—indeed scarcely any intelligent man can have failed to notice—a great recent change in the popular conception of a free government's duties and functions. When the middle-aged of our present generation were boys, the great majority of intelligent Anglo-Saxondom and all the wisest Liberals of the European continent accepted a theory of government which has sometimes been disparagingly called the "Policeman," but which may more properly be designated as that of *non-interference with the individual.* Lord Macaulay was one of its most distinguished advocates, and his illustrations of it are among the best known. According to it, the sixth, seventh, and eighth commandments were that part of the Decalogue with which the legislator and the magistrate had chiefly to do. Their business was *to protect property and person,* leaving to individuals all the liberty compatible with this general protection. The end of government was good roads and safe streets, cheap food and clothing, cheap and good education, not the enforcement of any moral or religious practices, the cultivation of special virtues, the protection of individuals against the consequences of their own acts.* Freedom in every sense—civil, religious, commercial—was the ideal toward which the progress of society tended. To such an extent was this theory recognized among ourselves, that the great political party then generally dominant might be said to have adopted it as a device; the party's official organ

---

* *Vide* Macaulay and Sydney Smith, *passim.*

hung out for its motto, "That government is best which governs least." But we were very little if at all in advance of the European Liberals. The "paternal" system of government, which wanted to do everything for the people and feared to let the individual take a step for himself, was generally scouted as a relic of a darker age. Even the English Conservatives, the successors of the Tories, were ashamed of it. The Continental Bureaucracy—felt, and felt heavily, in the smallest transactions of private life—was the standing bugbear and horror of all who were happy enough to live beyond its influence.

Such was the case twenty, or less than twenty years ago. *Nous avons changé tout cela.* The pendulum has swung the other way with a vengeance! The citizen of Massachusetts is now, in some respects, more restrained of his personal liberty than the subject of Louis Philippe then was; the former subject of that constitutional king is now living under the rule of an autocrat. England is not a country of rapid changes; but she has advanced—or backwarded—so far toward approval of interfering governments as to respect strong ones more than formerly. From among her distinguished literary men have arisen apologists for autocracy and palliators of Mormonism. Perhaps the climax was lately reached, when the editor of a standard English critical paper seriously held up the

Oriental polygamists and sodomites as models for Christendom.*

In short, that theory is rapidly becoming the popular one which maintains, in effect, that the best government governs most and is most felt in governing. The word *prohibited,*† which used to be the shibboleth of "paternal" rule, is becoming very familiar to republican citizens. Government is expected to prescribe what men shall eat and drink and wherewith they shall be clothed, to regulate the hours of labor, and distribute the profits of industry.

Merely as a matter of historical curiosity, this change would deserve examination. The best intellects have long speculated about the English Revolution of 1688, the French Revolution of 1789, the Age of Elizabeth, and the Age of Louis XIV. They are speculating yet, and the subjects are not yet exhausted. Our own epoch, however inferior it may be from a literary point of view, scarcely yields in political importance to any of these great eras. The

---

* See the 40th and 41st chapters of that singularly crude book, Mr. Hepworth Dixon's "New America." Perhaps, however, we ought not to wonder at this discovery, since the aquarians found out many years ago that Mohammed was wiser than Christ in respect of wine.

† *Defendu*, *Verboten*, the regular refrain of life in a great part of Continental Europe.

inversion of popular feeling which we are about to discuss would be interesting had it taken place in the last century.

But it is something more than a subject of curiosity. It is of the greatest practical importance to us. We are in the midst of the change. Our children are growing up under influences the very opposite of those which presided over our education. Are they, in this respect, more or less favored than we are? It is a vital question for them and for us. Investigation, in the first place, of the causes which have produced and are still producing this change in sentiment is to be desired, whatever view the inquirer may be predisposed to take of the change itself. He may hold, as I do, that it is a very decided step backward, or he may suppose, like many of our most active partisans, that it is a wonderful development in the direction of real progress; either way it is worth while to look for and into the springs of the movement. Without professing to constitute an exact science of history, we may suppose that some reason can be assigned for many, nay, for most of the great political events which take place, and that they are not all, as Mr. James Parton wisely supposes our late civil war to have been, a mere chapter of accidents.

Were a French critic of reputation to investigate

our social and political state, he might not improbably begin by telling us that all the phases of society which come up before our eyes in the daily papers and in every-day life: Beecher and Barnum, total abstinence and tariffs, the Jerome Park races and the eight-hour strikes, the ballets at the New York theatres and the college commencements all over the country, and twenty more things apparently without the slightest connection, may, every one of them, be shown to have their origin in the same leading ideas and forces, and their tendency toward the same end. I shall not profess or attempt to make so exhaustive an investigation, but only to trace some causes which are sufficiently obvious and sufficiently potent.

The first is doubtless *reaction*, an influence always ready to exert itself among people who have any intelligence, under governments that have any freedom, and therefore on both accounts especially powerful in our country. The non-interference theory, both here and in England, had been pushed to extremes, and had sometimes become a cloak for the selfishness of individuals and the weakness of rulers, particularly where large masses of capital were accumulated on the one side and herds of *prolétaires* on the other. Human nature, and common sense, and the laws of trade did not *invariably* arrange matters for the best. In such cases as infant labor and the lodging of city poor, some interference beyond the protection of liberty and property was found necessary.

This explanation in itself would probably seem a sufficient one to many persons—the pendulum has oscillated in one direction, it now oscillates in another; let it alone, it will come to an equilibrium in time—which makes a neat reference in a newspaper article, and is good enough as far as it goes, but really goes a very little way. True, it is highly important to us to know if the present inclination be to the right or the left, for good or for evil. The licentiousness of the court of Charles II. was a natural reaction from the tyrannical interferences of Puritanism: that did not make it proper or profitable. The dead conservatism which all over Europe succeeded the first Napoleon's fall was a necessary reaction from the convulsions which followed the French revolution: that did not make it a condition desirable to prolong. Let us then look further, and let us begin by investigating what may at first seem to have only a distant bearing on our subject—the parallel reaction that has been going on for fifteen years in favor of "strong" government, and material instead of intellectual dominion. To comprehend thoroughly the nature and scope of this movement, we must be fully impressed with the extent to which the purely intellectual element had prevailed in the politics of both hemispheres for some twenty years preceding the success of the second French Empire.

In these United States of America the sway of intellect, though not always intellect of the highest order, was almost supreme. Indeed, throughout a large portion of our country the physical man was shamefully ignored and neglected both publicly and privately. Our world was moved by speakers and writers. Many of our leading men had well-nigh lost the conception of physical force as a great political agency. The peaceful victories and revolutions of the ballot-box were the only ones which they could imagine possible. When the Rebellion broke out, they thought it *must* fail at once *because* it was unreasonable and illogical.

The national taste for field-sports saved the English from neglecting their physique; their national awkwardness and bashfulness prevented them from setting a high value on public oratory. But all their physical prowess had never inspired them with military tastes, and their comparative neglect of rhetoric tended to concentrate on their Press a remarkable amount of talent and learning: their commercial interests and heavy debt also contributed to make the English a peaceful and, therefore, an intellectually governed people. This impression of mental superiority over physical force lasted with them, as with us, quite into the new state of things. As late as 1858 Mr. Buckle was congratulating the world that the reign of Mars had nearly passed away, and that for a great war to be possible in future, one at least of the parties must be a semi-barbarous nation!

France, scarcely yet recovered from the exhaustion of the first Napoleonic wars, easily found a vent in Africa for her faintly renascent belligerency. Both the journalist's desk and the orator's tribune were greater political powers than the general's sword, and both were filled by the very first talent of the country.

All this was changed by Louis Napoleon's accession to power. It is a choice bit of popular cant to talk about the impotence of individuals in the present age. As an antidote to the exaggerated hero-worship of the Carlyle school, the notion may not be altogether mischievous; but as usually promulgated in its broadest sense it is equally unphilosophical and untrue, and the single example of the French emperor would be sufficient to disprove it. This one man, daring, able, lucky, and unscrupulous, caused a reaction all over the civilized world. There are very good reasons for supposing that his success tempted Jefferson Davis to prepare and attempt a *coup d'état* here. It was then that the idea of a great Southern Confederacy began to take definite form. In an embryo sort of way it had existed since 1832, and some of the conspirators had even held national offices ; but it had not masked itself in the guise of friendship, and its movements were comparatively open and honest. Davis himself was an avowed Secessionist, not a make-believe Unionist, in 1850. But after Louis Napoleon's triumphant usurpation, the brigands systematically entered the citadel in the disguise of servants, just as they had done in France. *Mutatis mutandis*, there was a great resemblance in the schemes. Louis Napoleon was elected to the presidency, a position which gave him the best chance of seizing supreme power. Davis could not get himself made president, but he could bully the cipher who was elected into giving him the cabinet office, which was more convenient for carrying out his plans than even the presidency would have been, and he could cause himself to be succeeded by a fellow conspirator. Louis Napoleon relied on the army for seizing power : on the army, together with the priests and the proletarian class, for maintaining himself in power. Our army was too small to intimidate the nation, and the clergy was geographically divided. Yet even amid these great differences we perceive a similarity of action. In the extent to which officers were tampered with, in the religious professions of Davis, and the almost unanimous adherence of the Southern clergymen to his cause, in the dependence placed on the "mean whites" of the South and the mobs of our Northern cities, we may recognize the American imitation of the European prototype.

Be this as it may, there can be no question about the great extent of the Emperor's influence in Europe. First, what was it on the country directly under his control?

The elder Napoleon was the foe of literary men, especially social and political theorists. He called them "ideologists" (whatever he meant by it), and tried to suppress them wherever his power extended. Such pen-work as he was obliged to have done, was done by scribblers of the lowest class, men like Barrère, who would hardly be admitted now-a-days to the columns of a Sunday newspaper. The nephew, who has, in more ways than one, profited by his uncle's mistakes, had no such insane hatred of intellect. He did not want a Barrère to do his more or less dirty work; he would have preferred a Guizot and a de Tocqueville. He was willing to make the position of great political and literary men pleasant, profitable, and even, as far as he could, honorable, if they would submit their wishes and plans to his. But this was precisely what the "illustrations" of the country would not do. Putting all patriotic and conscientious motives out of the question, ordinary self-respect would have prevented men, who had been powers in the State, from becoming his literary lacqueys. Hence, he was forced to take, both for his ministers and his journalists, second or third rate men. Now and then a young writer, like About, or a worn-out one, like Emile de Girardin, might coquet with the government; but it could command the entire services of none but inferior capacities. Finding that he did very well with these (thanks to the blunders of his enemies as well as his own ability and courage), the Emperor, strong in his six hundred thousand bayonets, grew more careless about the claims of intellect, and indifference easily passed into aversion. Officers were encouraged to bully and even assassinate literary men; and the young patricians whom the Emperor attached to his person and specially favored, were among the least intellectual of their set, distinguished for a sheer, unreasoning, bulldog courage.

To this reign of the sabre, both principle and interest placed the English in violent opposition. But their very hostility evinced their admiration, and amid all the invectives of their writers it was evident that they had been struck, if not terrified, by the brilliant and rapidly-achieved successes of the French autocrat. It was not merely that he had upset their European supremacy by fair means in the Crimea, and shattered the power of Austria in a sharp, short war. It was not that he had pocketed Savoy and Nice. The internal progress of France seemed to keep pace with the external. Her metropolitan improvements extorted the praise of those who most abhorred their contriver. All the insular self-sufficiency could not prevent British visitors from feeling that Paris had become the world's wonder for beauty and convenience; while London was the wonder of the world in another sense—for its unimproved and inartistic condition. The perfect organization of all departments, civil and military, impressed graver observers. The force of old traditions and principles and prejudices was partly broken down. A "strong-government" influence invaded and pervaded England, and, despite many of her ablest and most patriotic writers, the political demoralization and reaction went on, till they culminated in the general favor accorded by the upper and literary classes to our own "Great Rebellion."

To recent events in Germany a bare allusion is necessary, since they are so recent that the work (elsewhere) was already done. It is merely worth while to notice, in passing, how Bismarck's triumph shows that the German mind also was prepared for the reign of force.

In our own country the apparent effect of Louis Napoleon's success was, to provoke opposition and diminish somewhat our old friendship for France. But—putting aside the inspiration of Davis, which is only a matter of probable conjecture—it cannot be denied, by any candid and well-informed observer, that, amid all the continually recurring popular panegyrics of free institutions, a combination of circumstances had, for several years before the war, been shaking the republican faith of many, and those not the worst or most ignorant of the community. The innumerable errors and villainies in our municipal administrations (generally worse as the city is larger, and culminating in the corruptions of our largest and most metropolis-like city), brought unfavorable comparisons to the minds of those who remembered or had heard of the splendors and comforts of Paris. The sway of intellect was breaking down. The general spirit of lawlessness, engendered by slavery and fostered by the pro-slavery party at the North, inspired quiet people with a feeling of distrust and insecurity. Nor, though the strangely-styled "Democrats" were foremost in this lawlessness, could they be said to have altogether a monopoly of it; the Republicans were at least inclined to break the laws, if they did not always put their wishes into execution. The Central Government, too, was growing weaker and weaker under the nonentities who pretended to administer it. While Jeshurun waxed fat and kicked, while the popular mind was intoxicated with ideas of boundless wealth and dominion, thoughtful men hesitated and trembled, and foresaw, as through a glass darkly, an impending catastrophe. The fears of some were not unmingled with hope. The soul-crushing influences of arbitrary government, its destruction of all that is honorable in the individual man and woman—these evils were overlooked in view of its apparent public utility, its conservation of law and order.

While this influence was undermining us from one side, another power was growing in the Far West, the mention of which, after the French Empire, may at first strike the reader as a ridiculous anti-climax. But we cannot regard the Mormons as contemptible, when we consider what an impression they have made on very able Europeans. If they had only attracted the attention of such men as the able but eccentric and perverse Burton, or Mr. Hepworth Dixon, the confusion of whose moral ideas is only equalled by that of his style, we might pay little heed to them, but there are others who cannot be lightly passed over. And though I believe none of our own people have ever openly taken up the cudgels for Brigham Young, a sort of involuntary admiration for his organizing ability may frequently be detected in the reports of travellers. Men coming from a dangerous journey between the almost equal risks of starvation and murder, from regions where it is considered an excellent jest to stop a mail-stage by firing after it, and a man killed by mistake is rather a joke than otherwise, were pleased with the contrast of a community living in material plenty, under a regular though despotic system, and became half inclined to pardon the retrogression towards Oriental semi-barbarism.*

It is worth our while to notice, in this connection, that the success of these autocratic and despotic examples was mainly a *material* success. In the case of the Mormons it was altogether such. Brigham Young from the first discouraged colleges and all higher intellectual appliances, and the literary performances of his sect are of the weakest and most contemptible description. In the case of the French Empire the materialism was comparative. No one, with any knowledge in the premises, will deny that the French still maintain a high literary position—

* The Mormons are Orientals in more ways than one—unless our own "Gentiles," who come in contact with them greatly abuse the traveller's privilege. Have their European apologists never heard of the assassinations, mutilations, and other crimes, currently attributed to the "Saints," or do they consider the evidence of these crimes insufficient?

that the current literature of France is infinitely above our own, for instance. But the new celebrities of Louis Napoleon's time are not, on the whole, by any means equal to the old ones of Louis Philippe's; and all the greatest intellectual force, except that expended in fiction and the drama, is opposed to the Government.

Now this kind of success was exactly calculated to effect our popular mind, because the material progress of our country had turned the public attention that way, and weakened the hold of intellect in its more settled portions.

While these influences were thus working, our civil war broke out. For a moment national existence trembled in the scale. It really seemed as if we were going to destruction for want of those very things, the absence of which had been our chief boast—a standing army, taxation, checks on the press and the right of public assembly, centralization of the executive power, etc., etc. And though a magnificent uprising of the people put down the one great danger, our preservation was only accomplished by great deviations from both our theoretical and our practical standard. Dictatorial power was intrusted to the President, unrepublican measures (like conscription) were resorted to; in short, the Government was pretty effectually *strengthened,* with more regard to safety than consistency. And in this respect there has been no alteration or reaction since the close of the war, but rather the reverse; and one department of the Government has gone on strengthening itself by practically absorbing the other two. And as the less is apt to follow the greater, this new taste for strong government shows its pervading influence by some queer social demonstrations. Last year the school teachers, in various places, as if by common consent, took to threshing their pupils without much consideration for age or sex, till it looked as if the implements of torture, banished from their old quarters at the South, had taken refuge in the North and West.

But now it may be asked, What connection has this general change of feeling in favor of strong government with the tendency to government interference? It is true that the two ideas overlap at many points, and there seems an obvious analogy between them; but then there are other points where they completely diverge. There is nothing like Aquarian or Sabbatarian legislation in Continental Europe—scarcely anything in Western Europe, at least—which can fairly be brought under the head of sumptuary legislation at all. Nay, do we not find that the tendency of strong governments abroad is rather *not* to interfere with personal liberty in all matters unconnected with politics or religion?

This is true. The reaction in favor of strong government goes but a little way to explain the reaction in favor of interference. The former was converted into the latter by another potent spirit—the Puritan element.

Probably no other social and political principle—not even the Church of Rome—has ever been extolled with more fulsome panegyric on one side, and decried with more virulent invective on the other, than Puritanism ; and there are few contests of equal importance respecting which it can truly be said that *both* sides are so much in the right. Not merely that they are equally sincere (though, of course, with some hypocrites in both camps), but that their contradictory and seemingly opposite statements contain a large portion of positive truth. It is the old story of the two knights with the shield between them. The panegyrists have regarded the Puritan's conduct towards himself, while powerless to control others ; the detractors have looked at his conduct to others, when able to put them under his own rule.

It is of the greatest value to a nation that it should include among its citizens a body of men who are always thinking about and striving for their own civil and religious liberty, and who at the same time carry out the idea of God's kingdom on earth, according to their best comprehension of it, into their daily life.

When the French all but extirpated the almost identical Huguenot element, they inflicted a lasting and probably irreparable injury on their political liberty and social morality. So long as he is properly checked and tempered by other ingredients, the Puritan is a most precious member of society ; but give him the upper hand completely, let him have the supreme power, and he becomes one of the most fearful nuisances that ever went to and fro on the earth.

Not satisfied with being righteous himself, he insists on making all his neighbors righteous, by force if necessary, after his own fashion. He *will* cut all their social coats according to his moral cloth. A petty provincialism, a narrowness of ethical vision, has always been a marked trait of the Puritan character. His Mrs. Grundy is a village gossip. And this is why Puritanism is so specially distasteful to men of cosmopolitan experience. There is something provincial in its essence, and the Puritan can scarcely travel out of his circle and enlarge his knowledge of men and things without sensibly modifying his more salient peculiarities in spite of himself as it were, and often without his own knowledge. Our best journalists have exposed the fallacy of trying to deduce the government of a great city from that of a small village ; but the principle is much wider in extent, and lies at the root of nearly the whole system of interference. There is hardly a country doctor in New England but considers himself qualified to give advice to all the world and his wife about everything. The Puritan, meddling with other men's occupations, whether serious or sportive, has often been satirized. Two sayings respecting it deserve especial mention and remembrance,—Macaulay's, that the Puritan hated bear-baiting, not because it gave pain to the bear, but because it gave pleasure to the spectators; and Charles Leland's, that a New Englander's idea of hell was a place where every one had to mind his own business.

As long as this spirit of interference is kept within bounds, as long as this moral Quixotism is confined to the use of moral means, it cannot be said to do any positive harm; on the contrary, it is rather productive of good,—first, because its vagaries furnish amusement to better-regulated minds; secondly, because almost anything that provokes ethical discussion is so far praiseworthy. Intellectual motion is as necessary to a free community as tides are to the sea, and we can scarcely imagine a form of the eristic element which is not beneficial. But when it gets supreme control of the civil power, it becomes one of the most irritating and tormenting tyrannies that the evil wit of man ever devised. A political autocracy is not necessarily brutal and ignorant; and if it be neither, all those who are not specially earnest and serious in their pursuit of freedom and their moral purpose of life (that is to say, a large majority of mankind) can live along under it very tolerably. Multitudes make themselves quite comfortable in France. For those who have saved a portion of their property, and are not frightened out of their wits by the grimaces of Thaddeus Stevens, life under the military government now supreme at the South is by no means insupportable, and its principal annoyances are due to social interference rather than political subjugation. Autocratic oppression is neither universal nor constant : it weighs on particular persons at certain times,—as in a country whose wild beasts are not exterminated, a tiger now and then carries off some unfortunate. But the supremacy of a Puritan majority is felt by every individual in the minority, every week, every day, every hour of his life. It is like enveloping a whole community in musquitos.

On examining nations, or political parties, or almost any large collections of men, we are often struck by startling contradictions, of which the most acute philosophy can hardly find a satisfactory explanation. Nominally, the Puritan system abounds in the most self-sacrificing elements of the Christian scheme. Judging by the more respectable of their religious papers, and still more by the books which they write and recommend for children, a stranger would set them down for the meekest, mildest, best-tempered, least self-asserting of men, or at any rate for men who recognized the vital importance of these qualities; whereas, we find them in their own practice among the most arrogant and obstinate of mortals, generally regardless of the rights of others, and nearly as overbearing as the Romish Hierarchy. The fact is, that the Puritans inculcate on their children and inferiors the precepts of the New Testament, while they prefer to take the Old, and the most questionable parts of the Old, as the model for their own conduct.*

During the great agitation which culminated in war, the Puritans, shrewd enough, as usual, when their own liberty was at stake, flocked under the national banner. And so this restless, domineering sect, or combination of sects, became the leading and controlling element in the dominant po-

* The Judaism of the Puritans and of Calvinists generally is manifest in many ways—*e. g.*, by their use of that very contradictory expression, *the Christian Sabbath.*

Of course, it is not pretended that all upholders of the interference system are Calvinists, or *vice versa.* Some of the worst interferists can hardly be said to have any religion at all. But, as a general rule, the interference faith in politics and the Calvinistic faith in religion are found together.

litical party. The reaction in favor of strong government chimed in precisely with its ideas of personal interference, and gave to the latter their most active and oppressive form. Many circumstances connected with the war helped on this fusion.

First, the ignorance of other political subjects which the long agitation of the slavery question had brought about. This was particularly the case with regard to all matters of political economy. In regard to such knowledge our people were more backward in 1865 than in 1835. It was not merely that they could not attend carefully to these topics during the war, though that is certainly one reason. All manner of swindles and impositions spring up and thrive during a great conflict, as thieves are busiest when a city is in flames. Thus we may reasonably suspect that the preoccupation of the public mind about slavery contributed to the enactment of the New England Prohibitory Laws; and may feel quite sure that the Morril Tariff and its immediate successors slipped through Congress under cover of the war-cloud. A man engaged in a deadly struggle for his life is not exactly able to keep a sharp eye on his bank-account or his right of way. But this was not all. The present generation fairly forgot what they had learned or begun to learn as boys and young men. When, a little more than two years ago, the American Free-

Trade League was founded, an official position in it led me to ventilate the subject among my friends and acquaintances, comprising many well-educated and intelligent men. The ignorance which I found on every side was a source of daily astonishment to me. I don't mean that those with whom I conversed had wrong notions on the matter; they positively had none at all. Though this ignorance was most striking in subjects directly politico-economic, it was equally mischievous in several others; for instance, men having become accustomed to expect danger to their liberty from a single quarter, could not see that it might be in great peril from influences not oligarchic.

After the war, the disciples of Interference, who nearly all belonged to the victorious party, were tempted on by the intoxication of victory. Metaphor is indeed a copious source of fallacy, but it is also at times the most forcible way of expressing truth. The most violent of the Republicans were as literally drunk with success as ever man was with wine. And while the good sense of a large portion of their own party, and the possible though doubtful resurrection of the opposition, kept some feeble check upon them in the North, at the South they had *carte blanche*, an unlimited field open for experiment. For whatever may be the theoretical *status* of the Southern States (and it would be difficult, perhaps impossible, to form a consistent one), they were practically conquered territory—that is, the Congressional majority could do with them pretty much what it pleased. Mr. Stillé's pamphlet, *How a Free People conduct a Long War*, was widely read, and did good service at an important crisis. I think a neat sequel to it might now be written on the theme, *How a Free People are Sold after a Long War*,—a sequel which should draw a lesson, as he did, from British history, and show how, for fifteen years after the fall of Napoleon, every possible abuse, in church and state, was defended on the plea that a Tory government had put down Bonaparte, and saved England from being made a French province.

Thus the meddling, narrow, and intolerant Puritan spirit found itself possessed of almost unlimited political power, and encouraged by a general reaction in favor of "strong" government and anything that resembled it. Interference was, moreover, specially stimulated by the partial success and apparent triumph of the so-called "Temperance" agitation. Although this movement, originally inspired by the purest motives, had accumulated about it so much that was bad, as to have virtually lost its moral elements, and become a mere political engine, even before it appealed to force, still it retained the name and semblance of a great moral agitation; and though its achievements, since it had resorted to penal legislation, were more specious than real, and what in reality there was in them had been accomplished at the expense of much public demoralization in other ways, still the superficial record of the Maine or Prohibitory Laws was encouraging to the belief that men might be made moral and virtuous by vote of a majority, and perfect Christians by legislative enactment. The appearance, not only of drunkenness, but of drinking, had been abolished in several States : might not all other possible vices and misdemeanors be similarly put down by positive law ?

Thus a number of causes were at work in the same direction. But now came in another, which had been operating nearly as long as the slavery agitation, though, unlike that, it had sometimes slipped out of sight. We are apt to reject with scorn the notion of borrowing political ideas from foreigners, and boast rather of being able to influence the Old World. Yet it is certain that many vicious ideas of Old World origin flourish rankly among us. Those of the French, especially, translated, diluted, and modified, make way here, as in other countries, with many who are ignorant of their origin, and with some who might repudiate them if they knew it. The doctrines of French Socialism, borrowed and advocated by Greeley and others, had frequently been rejected by the popular common sense ; but the snake, often scotched, was never quite killed. After the war it started into new life, stimulated and revived by the field for agrarian operations opened in the newly reconquered territories. Now the system of Socialism rests on interference more than any other form of government or society short of sheer despotism. It was a reaction against the (real or supposed) oppression of the poor by the rich, the lower classes by the upper; and, accordingly, from the first attacked all that was eminent or peculiar, and strove to set the lowest kind of work above the highest. So that one of its chief bases is the principle of the handicap applied to legislation; and this, as we shall hereafter have occasion to observe in detail, also lies at the bottom of interference.

Such appears to me the *rationale* of the reaction in favor of unlimited governmental interference with the individual. First, a reaction all over the civilized world in favor of strong government, of which change the ability, courage, and unscrupulousness of a single man may be assigned as the prominent cause; then the Puritan spirit of intermeddling, identifying itself with the most active portion of our dominant party; next, a special impetus given to interference by the particular case of aquarian legislation; lastly, the more secret workings of foreign-born Socialism. I do not pretend to say that this explanation is wholly satisfactory. It may be affirmed, on the one hand, that the natural reaction of sentiment arising from the insufficiency of the "policeman" theory in some extreme cases and crises is sufficient to account for the change, and that any further speculations are superfluous. On the other hand, it is quite possible that my enumeration may err from defect rather than excess. Great political and social movements are so complex, that it is difficult to trace all their springs with accuracy. But I did not think it right to discuss the grave tendency which is our theme, without trying to throw some light on its origin; and the preceding explanation is that which appeared to be the most reasonable.

CHAPTER II.

Errors of Interference.

Interference contrary to the tendency of modern civilization and progress.—Its being the act of a majority does not alter this fact.—It logically leads to a State Church.—Presses on the poor more than on the rich.—Demoralizes the community in various ways: by confusing the distinction between real and technical crime: by familiarizing with falsehood those who advocate it: by introducing the handicap principle into economics and morals: by misplacing responsibility.

HAVING thus endeavored to get at the causes and antecedents of the Interference reaction, we have now to investigate the character of that movement, and determine whether it be for good or evil. But here two difficulties arise.

In the first place it is not easy to approach the subject with due equanimity and in a proper Christian frame of mind. Any one who has read and considered with the slightest approach to attention the vast and costly sacrifices made by good and great men in every age for freedom, and the enormous price which we ourselves have just paid to protect it, is moved to unbounded indignation at the bare thought that this precious temple should be nibbled away by vermin or pulled down by chattering apes—that his own fellow-citizens, supposed to be nothing more than his equals in the eye of the law and by the theory of our government, should constitute themselves

"Kings and kaisers, knights and popes,"

and exercise despotic authority over the most trivial and minute occurrences of his life. In the conflict between his emotions and his duty he feels like echoing the words of Panurge: "Page, my darling, take my hat and go down into the court and swear half an hour for me; I'll do as much for you another time." If I were disposed to take a leaf out of the interferists' book (which Heaven forbid!), and adopt their theory of social rights,* I should say that they ought to be summarily put down for causing reasonable men to lose their temper, and placing decorous men under strong temptation to use bad language.

The second impediment is the choice of materials in the *embarras de richesses* which presents itself. When any one, not a fool or a fanatic, seriously contemplates the effects of this transplanting of petty despotism into democracy, his difficulty is, not what to say, but what not to say. Ex-Governor Andrew, in

---

*As expounded by the Secretary of an English "Alliance." See *Mill on Liberty*, p. 160, English edition. Quoted also by Ex-Governor Andrew.

his *Errors of Prohibition,* has occupied nearly a hundred and forty pages in treating of one branch of our topic ; and very few of his sentences can be accused of prolixity or irrelevancy, while there are various pregnant hints in them that might easily be expanded into chapters. I understand that a single weekly paper (*Wilkes' Spirit*) published several columns a week for several weeks on the New York license law; and allowing three-quarters of this to have been mere rubbish (as it probably was), there would remain pertinent matter enough to make a fair-sized pamphlet on *one subdivision of one branch.* The literature of the economic division alone, or those questions in which morals occupy a very subordinate position—*e. g.*, that of free trade—would make a small library.

These prefatory observations are deemed necessary to excuse any harshness of expression, or abruptness of transition, or omission of intervening steps, which the reader may remark.

Perhaps the first objection to the Interference theory, which would naturally present itself to any man having even a superficial acquaintance with history, is that it is contrary to the general tendency of modern civilization and progress. The freedom of the individual, as we moderns understand it, was almost unknown to the ancient world in practice and utterly repudiated in theory. To tell a Greek philosopher that the political society called the State was made for the benefit of its individual members, would have seemed to him an inversion of all correct system. His idea was just the other way, that the citizens were made for the benefit of the Government. Athens was in many respects a model ancient republic; yet there we find, on the one hand, a majority of the population slaves, and, on the other hand, the wealthiest citizens holding their lives and property by a very precarious tenure. All through the Middle Ages despotism was only tempered by anarchy, and the individual who enjoyed any freedom owed it to brute force and personal prowess. But from the quarrels of tyrants among themselves, and especially the disputes between churches and potentates, the rights of the people gradually gained means of expression, until the liberty of the individual was recognized as a principle in some countries. And the tendency of modern progress, though with occasional ebbs like the present, has flowed pretty steadily in this direction. Although the "social contract" failed to secure general acceptance as a proper theory of government, the idea has grown and established itself that society was made for the live individuals who compose it, not for the benefit of any single person or particular class, still less for the sake of a political abstraction. Religious persecution has become so faint, that we may almost speak of it as no longer existing. The kidnapping of a little Jew boy, a few years ago, raised a greater outcry throughout Christendom, than the extermination of a whole province of heretics would have caused two centuries earlier. There is more commercial freedom in France under the autocrat Louis Napoleon, than there was in England under the champion of liberty, William III. Serfdom has been abolished by one nation after another, till almost every civilized country has rid itself of the curse. Even under arbitrary governments, there is a progressive extension of education and suffrage, admission of the people to their rights, and preparation of them for those rights. But it is in our own land that the principle has been pushed to something very near its utmost limits. We have made the humblest member of the community eligible to its highest offices; we have proclaimed, both literally and virtually, *ad nauseam*, that every man is politically and civilly as good as his neighbor. Yet this political sovereign is to be reduced to a state of pupilage like a school-boy or an imbecile! How utterly absurd, that the man who is pronounced qualified to decide on the gravest national questions, perhaps to change the destinies of the world by his vote, shall not be deemed capable of regulating his own diet or of choosing a market in which to dispose of the fruits of his own industry! What is this but a repetition of the smallest and most contemptible follies of "paternal" government, as practised by absolute monarchs?

The only answer can be, that one set of acts emanate from the will of a single person, while the others are expressions, more or less direct, of the will of a majority. *But does that alter the character of the acts themselves?* Suppose in a community of two hundred thousand, one hundred and ninety thousand belong to the same church, and that by a unanimous vote they proceed to burn the other ten thousand as heretics; would the proceeding be any less a violation of humanity and religious liberty because it was the act of a majority? Or, if the ten richest men in the same community were seized and put to death and their property confiscated, merely because they were the richest men; would it make any difference to them or to justice whether the deed resulted from the ukase of a single despot or the other one hundred and ninety-nine thousand nine hundred and ninety? But we are supposing impossible cases. No, nothing is impossible to fanaticism! It is not amenable to the rules of ordinary logic, and, moreover, in this matter it would have logic on its side. Once admit the principle that it is right for Government (whether representing a majority or not) to interfere, on account of the inferred moral tendency of their acts, with the personal freedom of individuals who have committed no crime, and you cannot consistently stop short of a State Church. Do we not as Christians profess to believe that a man's eternal interests are more important than all others—that saving his soul is of more consequence than saving his body and his goods? Are we not supposed to hold that the highest and safest morality has its support, if not its origin, in our blessed religion? If Government ought to interfere with every man's private life under pretence of making him healthy or moral after its own pattern, *a fortiori* is it bound to regulate his religion? Have we, the majority, a right to prevent one citizen from drinking beer because it may encourage to get drunk on whiskey? and have we no right to check (what appears to us) the tremendous errors of Romanism or Socinianism? Verily, this is making meat more than the life, and raiment more than the body.

This is no new or forced aspect of the case. More than twenty years ago the question came up incidentally in England. A species of modern transcendental Tories (of whom Gladstone was then one) defended not only the Church "Establishment," but its right to control all the secular education of the country. This position was disputed by Macaulay and other Liberal leaders, whose chief organ was the *Edinburgh Review;*

and these able men founded their arguments on the hypothesis that the "policeman" theory of government was the correct one, that it was the business of civil rulers and legislators to protect life and property, not to supervise or dictate the morals and religion and education of the whole community. And they tacitly admitted that, conversely, the Interference theory led not merely to a State Church, but to a State religion of the most pervading and exacting kind.

It may be said, however, that this is a purely abstract speculation about a danger altogether imaginary, since the multiplicity of sects among us precludes any possibility of a dominant church anywhere. Now, I am not so sure of this. In the first place, allowing it to be *unlikely* that any one denomination will ever assume a decided preponderance in any of our new or reconstructed States, I do not see the *impossibility* of such an occurrence. But further, it is not necessary that the aggressive sect should constitute a majority: they need only be compact and energetic enough to influence a majority or turn the political balance. In our Empire State and Metropolitan City the Church of Rome has actually for some time enjoyed exclusive advantages and extorted large contributions from Protestant tax-payers for its benefit; yet the Romanists are probably not even a majority in the city, and certainly very far from one throughout the

State. Besides, there are certain outward formulas of Christianity in which pretty nearly all denominations agree, and it would need only a slight extra infusion of fanaticism to unite nearly all denominations in forcing them upon skeptics and unbelievers. One of these is the weekly attendance on divine service. Christians generally believe that public worship is not only a religious—that is, a theological—but a moral necessity : even those who have doubts about the utility of the sermon recognize the value of meeting for purposes of prayer and praise. And many of those who are not themselves regular in their attendance, admit the importance of that privilege, which indolence or other temptation leads them to slight. Nor can we say that the neglect of God's house is an evil of small extent. A popular, or once popular writer of the Tupper species, asserts that only one-third of the population of New England are regular church-goers. I am not aware on what statistics this assertion is founded, but supposing that it is within a hundred per cent. of the truth, we may form a shrewd guess at the proportion in other parts of the Union. Sabbatarian legislation of various kinds is not wanting, but the people do not seem to go to church any the more for being kept out of other places. Is it not our duty, on the Interference principle, to make them go? Surely, there is as much injury done to a man's soul by pertinaciously abstaining from all occasions of public worship as by drinking a glass of wine, and the example in the former case is at least as bad as in the latter.

And this, to my mind, is a decisive argument, and disposes of the whole question by the *reductio ad absurdum.* If you assume to take care of every man's morals, you must also take care of his religion. As the greater includes the less, the repudiation of a united Church and State ought to involve the rejection of the whole system of Interference. It may be objected, however, that this argument does not reach those interfering regulations in which the economic element is admitted to dominate over the moral, and which only inflict a pecuniary loss upon their victim without subjecting him to any personal restraint. Thus, it does not touch the iniquitous imposition of "Protection." We therefore proceed to another count in our indictment. There is no lack of them.

All the paternal, protective, prohibitive legislation with which we are harassed, is not only unjust in itself, but specially un-democratic and un-American, because it weighs more heavily on the poor than on the rich.

I should be one of the last to admit that a measure is necessarily bad because it runs foul of some democratic ideal. The strongest element in a government has a constant tendency to go on accumulating strength, and a slight drag upon it may at times be very desirable. But when the question is not one of limit or modification, but of positive opposition, when a measure or institution is thoroughly hostile to the broad principles on which our whole political fabric is founded, the case becomes very different. And thus is it with any law which bears unequally on rich and poor ; and of this class is all the legislation begotten of Interference.

Take a prohibitory liquor law. You shut up barrooms and forbid hotels from serving wine to customers. What does the rich citizen care ? He usually has two places of refuge—his club and his own house. Go further, suppress all retail traffic : he can afford to buy his wines wholesale. Carry out your fanaticism to its highest pitch ; inoculate all the United States with the prohibition mania, and forbid the manufacture of fermented liquors in the country. Even then he may escape you. He can fly to France or some other comparatively free country.

Or take Sabbatarian laws. You prohibit cars and steamboats from plying on Sunday. How does this affect the rich man ? He can hire a carriage. Close the livery stables on that day : he can afford to keep a vehicle of his own. Go to the scarcely possible length of making vehicular locomotion on Sunday penal. Still, the millionaire is hardly touched; for he is not bound to his work all the week; he can select another day for his out-door amusement. The inconveniences of Liquor Laws and Sunday Laws fall exclusively on the poor man.

The interference of Protection, though it affects all classes, touches the poor most severely. If a rich man has to pay fifty per cent. more than he ought for his clothing, he must only make two coats last him as long as three used to, or cut down some other luxury in proportion. But to the poor man fifty per cent. extra on his clothing, and that of his family, is a serious matter. Of many necessaries, such as the cheaper kinds of clothing, bedding, iron tools, and sewing-thread, the poor family consumes nearly as much as the rich, and the differenee of a large increase in their price to the two classes is the difference between taking half a story off a four-story house, and taking it off a one-story house.

There is, indeed, a class of interfering laws which affect the rich man more than the poor, indeed scarcely touch the latter at all. These are laws *strictly* sumptuary, enactments limiting personal expenses, simply as personal expenses;—laws, for instance, forbidding a citizen to inhabit a house of more than a certain size, or to drive more than a specified number of horses, or to wear garments of peculiar fabrics or values. Such legislation, at one period very common, has long been exploded in the Old World. Not many years ago it was feared that a species of unwritten law of this class might be framed in the New by popular opinion. The material luxury inseparable from the growth of large cities, has pretty well dispelled this fear, at least for the present. All the interfering statutes now in vogue, or likely to be for some time, strike the poor hard, and pass lightly by the wealthy.

Still, it may be urged that there is too much of mere theory and speculation in this argument, inasmuch as necessities (real or supposed) have led us frequently, during the last six years, to violate republican principles. I therefore proceed to another, resting directly on fact, and involving, under different forms, all the practical merits of the dispute.

Interfering legislation is wrong, because it demoralizes the community in various ways.

This is going to the root of the matter, meeting the enemy point-blank, carrying the war into Africa. For the greater part of Interfering legislation is founded on the assumption that Government ought to take charge of every man's private morality, for the purpose of protecting the public morality; and even in cases like that of Protection, where the economic element predominates, the moral element is also quite appreciable, since many Protectionists admit that, according to the rules of political economy, the case must go against them ; wherefore they take refuge in moral and patriotic motives.

Nor must we be astonished that men in pursuit of good ends should fall into evil. When legislation goes beyond its appropriate sphere, the better the men the worse their mistakes often are. And the errors of the best men are apt to be the most instructive. John Stuart Mill, in his justly-renowned essay on "Liberty," has protested with equal warmth and acuteness against the interference of governments in individual concerns. Yet, as if afraid of carrying out his own principles, he afterwards proceeds to admit and approves of some very arbitrary interferences in vogue on the European Continent—*e. g.*, the laws which forbid marriage unless parties can show that they have the means of supporting a family.* If Mr. Mill had chosen to investigate the practical working of this law in various parts of Germany, he would have seen that it produces no end of immorality in the shape of concubinage, and concubinage licensed by public opinion. If he had chosen to apply his powerful mind a little more closely to the regulation, I think he would have perceived its theoretical weakness. "Supporting a family." What *is* a family?

* Page 194—English edition.

Is it one child, or three children, or a dozen? How can it be told beforehand how many children the couple will have? Are they to be allowed to begin with a sufficiency for one child, and must they show a corresponding increase of means before every successive increase of family is lawful? The more we look at such a rule, the more it appears to us as absurd as it is oppressive—which, indeed, is a general characteristic of paternal, protective, and prohibitive legislation.

I repeat, then, emphatically, that Interference legislation demoralizes the community in various ways: that it must do so theoretically, that it does so practically.

First, by confusing the popular conception of law, and making men regard it as a mere matter of arbitrary enactment, without foundation in their consciences and feelings.

The experience of history has caused ethical students to receive, as something very like an axiom, this proposition: that the multiplication of *mala prohibita*, or technical offences, causes the mass of the people to ignore the distinction between them and *mala in se*, or actual crimes, which the impulses of civilized men generally agree in reprobating. Thus it would not be difficult to prove that prohibition of marriage with a deceased wife's sister causes a great deal of incest among the lower orders in countries where it is the law. Of course, our own prohibitionists expect to change all this. They hope, for instance, to make beer-drinking as disreputable as fornication is and falsehood ought to be; but until they can change human nature they will be disappointed.

Even actions allowed on all hands to be bad and justly punishable, may become objects of public sympathy when visited with punishment in excess of their desert. Less than a hundred years ago, women were hanged in England for shop-lifting, a species of petty larceny. Here the wrong done to the criminal by the punishment was evidently greater than the wrong done to society by the crime.

Next, we see *mala in se* popularly excused by their association with *mala prohibita*. The execution of women for shop-lifting, just mentioned, is an instance of the always great and sometimes exaggerated respect paid by the Anglo-Saxon mind to the rights of property; yet we find a doubtful character in more than one sense, Robin Hood, erected into one of England's traditional heroes; his example cast a glory about highway robbery which continued to gild it almost to the present day. Why was this? Because the followers of Robin Hood (whether he be a real person or an eponymous hero, a man or a myth) were political outlaws before they were bandits. It has often happened, and sometimes still happens, that in conquered and oppressed countries law becomes a synonym of wrong rather than of right.

Finally, let us eliminate the positive offence entirely, leaving only the technical—that is, men who have never committed any *malum in se*, are found guilty of *mala prohibita*. In this case the sympathy of all not directly engaged in passing and supporting the law will be with the violators of it, because the law is, from a moral point of view, arbitrary. Thus, very few persons consider smuggling, as constantly achieved by travellers, anything more than a venial sin. Common sense tells every man not infected with the Prohibition phrensy that selling a glass of beer or cider is not a crime in the same sense as theft or assault; and if he has intelligence and learning to reason out the matter, he sees that the proceeding is as illogical as it is oppressive. The first effect of his convictions is to lessen his respect for the makers of the law, though that is too mild a way of putting it. It would be nearer the truth to say that he regards them with abhorrence and disgust; and if not with contempt also, it is because they are too formidable to be safely despised. Gulliver could not afford to despise the insects of Brobdignag. The law having no moral force on the large number of persons opposed to it, continual attempts at evasion will naturally be made, and many of them will be successful. There is no evading a law against robbery or murder, except where robbers and cut-throats form a large part of the population, for to put down such crimes is the interest of every honest man; but in the case of this "paternal" legislation of Interference, the interests of a great number is the other way. And though the law may have been passed by the vote of a majority, still, as the majority are not likely to have so lively an individual interest in taking away the minority's liberty as the latter have in preserving it, they will not show the same individual energy in enforcing the law that the others practise in violating it. Moreover, there need not be, and very frequently is not, a *local* majority in favor of the law. The legislator must therefore have large recourse to the services of spies and professional informers; and this still further increases his unpopularity. The detective who tracks and traps the assassin or the forger is the bloodhound of the law, and is regarded everywhere with a certain fearful respect. The common informer is the mangy cur whom all men long to kick, while some would not be sorry to extend the same greeting to his employers.

Thus the legislation of Interference demoralizes the masses who oppose it, by confusing their ideas of wrong and right. But it also, in the second place, demoralizes those who promote it, by confusing their ideas of truth and equity.

The amount of positive falsehood which passes current among our modern Puritans ought to awaken more astonishment and indignation than it does. Whence they get it is a puzzle, for the old Puritans were certainly not remarkable for systematic and pertinacious violation of truth. Such untruths of theirs as have come down to us seem usually to have been hallucinations rather than inventions. But many of their descendants seem to have lost the perception and appreciation of truth as completely as the Irish Romanist, who, it is notorious, understands by truth whatever makes for his side, and by falsehood whatever makes against it. Is it possible that they ultimately owe this vice to the Irish among us, who first infected the democratic party with it, and the Republicans then caught it from the Democrats while striving to overbid them (as they have more than once done) with the baser elements of society? Or, if this be deemed too recondite an explanation, shall we say that outrageous falsehood is a necessary concomitant of violent partisanship, and that this is only another example of the folly of attempting to accomplish moral reforms by dragging moral questions into the dirty field of partisan warfare? Perhaps we may admit that both agencies had their share, and still leave room for a third explanation—namely, that the system of Interference, being founded on false principles, naturally looks to falsehood for its support, and that Protectionists and Prohibitionists have recourse to exaggeration, mendacity, and calumny for lack of serious arguments. Whatever the cause, the melancholy effect is palpable and salient.

One of the most recent and marked exhibitions of it was the nomination for Congress, as an Aquarian or so-called Temperance candidate, of P. T. Barnum, the notorious showman, whose whole life, by his own autobiographical confession* has been a career of unmitigated deception. A great many persons who professed and called themselves Christians, thought it decent and proper to uphold and recommend this lover of lies; and though he was unsuccessful, his bad character did not defeat him. There happened to be a party majority on the other side. The discussion on the Prohibition Law in Massachusetts, this year, brought out some of the loosest and wildest assertions imaginable. A witness, before the Special Committee of the Legislature, gravely stated that "the annual mortality from intemperance in the United States was fifty thousand."† Ex-Governor Andrew

* Which, considering its immoral tendency, should rather be called an ought-not-to-buy-ography.

† Errors of Prohibition, p. 112.

showed in black and white that the return of deaths from that cause, in 1860, was less than *one* thousand. This sample of Prohibition *facts* reminds one of Carlyle's saying that we must sometimes get up statistics, "not in the vain hope of acquiring knowledge, but to prevent other people's ignorance from being thrust upon us." It is equally notorious that the Prohibitionists raised the hue-and-cry against all who opposed them, and denounced as either a drunkard or a friend of drunkenness every man who did not support the hourly interference of Government in the diet of individuals. They invented the tasteful and decorous name of "rummy" wherewith to stigmatize their opponents. To be sure, persons who are proud to call themselves *teetotlers* (I am not sure how the word is spelled—any way is good enough for it) cannot be expected to apply very elegant epithets to their antagonists.

Some of the Prohibitive legislation is avowedly founded on assumptions which are sheer falsehoods—*e. g.*, that lager bier is an intoxicating liquor. It is not such in any natural or rational sense of the words. Under exceptional circumstances it may produce a slight exhilaration ; so may soda-water, tea, animal food, or even fresh air and sunshine. The Protectionists really hate light beers and wines, because they do *not* habitually produce intoxication, and thus invalidate their sweeping assertions.

The moral and economical lines of our question overlap here, as at many other points. Prohibition and Protection go consistently together, and the perfection of mendacity and malignity, of carelessness about truth and calumny against persons, may safely be looked for in any organ of both these forms of Interference—the *New York Tribune*, for instance. The manner in which this newspaper wages warfare against those who oppose its pet systems of Interference, is simply to lie about them as hard as it can. Out of a multitude of examples which might be given, we need only take as a specimen its random and frantic vituperation of the American Free-Trade League. If there ever was an Association eminently respectable and honest in its origin, it was that League. Its founders belonged, in about equal proportions, to the two great political parties, but none of them were party leaders, and few of them politicians at all. Their general pecuniary position was that of men too rich to be bought, and not rich enough to buy others. They were not seeking fortune, or office, or notoriety. That the *capacity* of such a body should be attacked was perfectly natural, since it is a current popular delusion that no man is fit to give an opinion on public affairs unless he has dragged through years of dirty caucus work; but there was no excuse for assailing their integrity. The *Tribune*, however, having ascertained that out of more than thirty officers of the League, five or six had some business connection with England, immediately set up a howl that all its officers were bought agents of the English manufacturers. This abominable lie it repeated day after day (possibly is repeating still), and the falsehood found a ready echo in other Protectionist journals throughout the country, and on the floor of Congress. It is worth while noticing, in the present connection, that this paper, the *Tribune*, has always been anxious to destroy the faint shadow of assistance which our laws still profess to give to the individual slandered by the journalist.

It may be said that these calumnies are only the ordinary amenities of partisan warfare. But they are most certainly not the necessary and inseparable results of partisanship, as the example of other well-known and influential political prints clearly shows. The palliation, at best, amounts to this, that these Interferists, under pretence of promoting public morality, not only meddle with private liberty, but do so by employing the worst devices of the worst class of party hacks. Can there be any reasonable doubt as to the effect of such proceedings upon their own nature?

Thus we have seen that the legislation of Interference demoralizes both sections of the community—that which suffers under the law, and that which inflicts it. But it demoralizes the whole community in another way—by the introduction of the handicap system into both economics and morals.*

I do not know how far the progress of the turf among us may have familiarized general readers with the meaning of the technical term *handicap.* It is a race in which horses of all merits compete, and the best are so heavily weighted as to put them on an equality with the worst. The worst horse, not the best, is made the standard; and the results of the running are as unnatural—that is, as little in accordance with the natural capacity of the horses—as can well be imagined. Now this is exactly the principle on which all the Interference legislation reposes, for it restrains the natural capacities and developments of its subjects, and makes the worst of them its standard instead of the best.

Thus, the eight-hour law is an attempt to measure the physical capacity and industrial perseverance of the best workmen by those of the worst. The Pro-

* As some of my readers may possibly have seen something like this before, it is proper to say that an article on Handicap Legislation, which appeared in the *Round Table* this summer, was written by me.

tective system insists on regulating the price of commodities, not by what it costs to produce under the most favorable, but by what it costs to produce them under the least favorable circumstances. Socialism, as we have already had occasion to remark, is prone to these absurdities; because its essence is to set the lower kind of work above the higher—of which we find a good illustration in Greeley's assertion, that a man who can raise potatoes is better educated than one who knows Greek and Hebrew. Hence, Socialists are usually Protectionists, and Interferists generally.

The moral handicap of Interference is not quite so obvious as the economic, to the hasty observer; but it comes out clearly enough on a little examination. It usually takes the form of the argument against temptation. "You must not drink that claret."—"Why not? I believe it is good for me, and my doctor tells me to drink it; and as to drunkenness, a child of fourteen might take a pint of that wine and water with impunity."—"Perhaps so; but your neighbor, Paddy O'Rafferty, *will* get drunk if there is a drop of liquor in the country: it is necessary to remove this temptation from him; *therefore*, nobody in the country shall drink anything that can by any possibility be supposed capable of intoxicating!" Were this principle carried out into all the departments of life, it would cause a very general shutting up shop, and bring society nearly to a stand-still. If there is no liquor in the place, there can be no intoxication. Certainly; and if there are no women, there can be no fornication; if there is no property, there can be no theft; if there are no books or periodicals printed, there can be no lies printed. But this, though a very fair *reductio ad absurdum* of the Interference principle, is not what I am now urging, neither will I dwell on the set-off pointed out incidentally by Mill—namely, that persons of independent and antagonistic natures are roused to opposition by such laws. What I insist on is the inversion of all ethical logic, the utter injustice of taking as a basis of legislation the presumed needs of the lowest, and weakest, and worst members of society. If Paddy O'Rafferty is unable to control his appetite for liquor, if you consider his life so valuable that Government is bound specially to interfere in the case, shut *him* up, punish *him*. Why meddle with me, and my family, and my friends, and all the respectable people in the neighborhood? Why try us by his standard, and judge of our temptations by his? May I not walk in Broadway, because Lovelace insulted a lady there last night? May I not enter Tiffany's shop without a guard of two policemen, because one of the swell-mob tried to steal a diamond ring the other day? Carry out the principle, and you will end in a government for which (happily) no language has as yet found a name, but which might not unaptly be expressed by the term *Cacocracy*. For it would be a government, not indeed necessarily administered by the vilest members of the community, but based upon the real or presumed moral requirements of the very worst subjects under its jurisdiction.*

But there is still another way, analogous to the last, in which Interference legislation on moral questions demoralizes the community. It transfers and mis-

---

* Several years ago I was staying with a very excellent friend of mine, a college professor. He excused himself for not offering me wine at dinner, because a drunken student had killed one of the tutors in a row. I could not then and have never since been able to see the connection. But the moral of the incident is worth noting. Some years later I went to stay with my friend again. He produced a bottle of wine after dinner. His doctor had ordered him to drink it.

Interferists say that it is selfish for a man to indulge in that which tempts others to excess. Perhaps it is; but at any rate the selfishness is not all on one side. What name shall we give to the feeling which prompts a man to deprive his neighbors of their necessaries and comforts, in order to remove from himself the temptation which he is bound to resist? And in what terms shall we characterize the attempt to make men unselfish by dint of legislation?

places responsibility, calling one man to account, not only for another man's action, but for another man's different action.

If A abstains from drinking wine lest B hurt himself by drinking whiskey, though the logic of the proceeding may not be transparent to all, the motive is doubtless good; at any rate, it is no one's business but A's. But that A should hinder C from drinking wine lest B injure himself by drinking whiskey, is an equal inversion of logic and equity. The whole merit of the sacrifice consists in its being voluntary; the absence of the voluntary element converts it into intolerable oppression. Sydney Smith ridiculed the pretended benevolence of some persons, by putting it into this formula: *A, seeing B's distress, is irresistibly moved to make C give him something.* But there is no need of caricature here. We have only to state the fact. *A, seeing the mischief which B works for himself and others by doing something, is irresistibly impelled to prevent C from doing something else.*

A proper sense of responsibility is one of the essential foundations of morality, and every erroneous distribution of responsibility tends to sap the community's moral sense. In uncivilized and unsettled countries this erroneous distribution is of constant occurrence. When the king of the Cannibal Islands has the belly-ache, he brains the first of his subjects on whom he can lay hands. When a Western gambler has lost his money, he is apt to stab or shoot the first stranger whom he encounters. One of the leading characteristics of law, and order, and civilization, and true progress, is the proper tracing and placing of responsibility,—"putting the saddle on the right horse," according to a familiar phrase. It is the difference between an African ordeal and a trial by judge and jury. An arbitrary shifting of responsibility is odious to men, nearly in proportion to their advance in civilization, and if reduced to a sort of system, it will go no little way toward uncivilizing them.

It is the habit of shallow philosopherlings to get hold of half-truths and use them at random; to take principles by the wrong end and dislocate them fearfully by mishandling. Various social and political influences have long prevented the lower classes of most European countries from getting a fair start and fair play in the race of life. Hence, some serious and many sentimental moralists started the idea of social responsibility for the acts of the individual. In one sense it contained a great deal of truth, and that not with regard merely to the poorest and most obscure *prolétaires*; but the Interferists misconstrued it, and regarded the responsibility not as binding the individual and society *solidairement*, but as transferred to other individuals. Thus there can be no reasonable doubt that the American public is partly responsible for the sins of the *Herald* and the *Tribune*, since it has made the editor of the one journal a millionaire, and the editor of the other a political personage ; but it would be a most unreasonable and unfair inference, that all the newspapers in the country ought to be made subject to a government censorship. Yet this is exactly the principle of the Prohibition laws. There exists a species of ferocious philanthropy, professed by many French and some Anglo-Saxon writers—the late Horace Mann afforded a good specimen of it—which runs a muck at every quiet, respectable, minding-his-own-business citizen, for the evil which he does *not* do, and which they have never been able to show him clearly how he might prevent. If society has not been just to any of its members, it should endeavor to remedy the injustice—first, by looking after the improvement of their physical well-being, and then by judiciously stimulating their mental and moral capacity ; instead of which the tendency of Interference is to worry and aggravate them by diminishing their sources of enjoyment, while at the same time it attempts to make scapegoats of those among the more favored classes who have the misfortune to dissent from the ethical dogmas of a temporary, perhaps accidental and fictitious majority.

CHAPTER III.

The Prohibition Stage of the Aquarian Movement.

Importance of the subject.—Prestige in favor of Aquarianism.—Why fallacious.—Threefold division of the question.—Absurdities of the Aquarians on the Biblical argument: On the physiological.—The moral police argument: Statement of it: Its results shown by application of the principle to the treatment of other vices, licentiousness, gambling, falsehood, and slander.—Appeal to Aquarians.

WE have already had occasion to remark (what indeed must be obvious on slight reflection) that the laws inspired by the principle of Interference are of two kinds: the one sort, like "Protective" enactments, merely mulct their victim in a pecuniary sum, or operate as an unjust tax; the other sort, like Aquarian or Sabbatarian legislation, directly attack his personal freedom and comfort. Of this latter class, the Prohibitive development of the movement, loosely called "temperance," more precisely "total abstinence," vulgarly "tetotal," "teetotal," and "T-total," and which may most correctly be styled *Aquarian* (since it aims at the suppression of all ordinary beverages except water), is so important as to deserve and require a separate notice. Since the ascetic tendency of early Christianity (like which, it originated in a reaction against rampant vice), no moral agitation has been so formidable in its proportions or so perilous to individual liberty.

This movement, I repeat it, in its present stage, is fraught with the gravest peril to the personal liberty of the individual; for whenever anything bad, whether proposed measure or established institution, has on its side a large number of men who are, or are reputed to be, good, it is on that account tenfold more dangerous. Wherefore it is better to begin by disposing of this prestige.

There are a great many "good men," clergymen, church communicants, respectable citizens, etc., etc., in favor of Aquarianism, and so much in favor of it that they are willing to go to the length of enforcing it by civil penalties. Very well. This amounts to a *prima facie* evidence in its favor, strong *prima facie*, if you will, but *prima* facie only. It is like good character at a trial. The prisoner at the bar has a good reputation, but if crime is clearly proved against him, what does his previous reputation avail? Some maintain that it positively aggravates his guilt. So, conversely, with the argument drawn from the fact that many bad and corrupt men, New York democratic politicians, etc., are opposed to Aquarianism. The reign of the Patlander is the one thing under God's heaven worse than the reign of the Puritan, and those who have suffered under the former may be pardoned for committing themselves blindly to the latter. Still, let us bear in mind that this, too, is merely *prima facie*, and that the old maxim, *Noscitur a socio,* is not necessarily true in all cases.

It is of course a great point for a partisan if he can attach bad or unpopular associations to what he opposes. Thus, Protectionist journals are always "hoarsely bawling," *British* Free-Trade! But suppose we say British Free Speech, British Free Press, British *Habeas Corpus.* All these are British, as much as Free-Trade is.

Suppose that in any country (as has happened in some modern countries) the people should abolish and persecute Christianity. Then the Romanists and Protestants of that country would be in the same boat as regards the majority. Or suppose (as has also sometimes happened) there was a Romanist majority bent on stifling all free discussion, and a minority composed of Protestants and skeptics; that minority would naturally unite against the dominant party. How unfair it would be to charge the Protestants with Romanism in the former case, or with infidelity in the latter!

Besides, when we come to scrutinize the goodness of those who support penal Aquarian legislation, we shall probably find that, so far as it exists, it exists in spite, not in consequence of their Aquarianism, which makes them very careless of truth, and equally regardless of their neighbors' rights. When Buckle propounded his curious paradox, that civilization owed everything to intellect and nothing to morals, and illustrated his position by the crimes of bigots, Goldwin Smith indignantly denied the goodness of bigots. Without going so far as the ex-Professor, we may safely question the *thorough* goodness of a fanatic, however free from sensual vices, or eminent for what are called business virtues.

Once more: if those who are carried away by an array of names would only extend their vision beyond one portion of one country, and take into account the multitudes of great and good men all over the civilized world who are in the daily habit of using fermented liquors, they might see how much this prestige amounts to. But here comes in the overweening, unbounded, illimitable conceit of the narrow-minded Puritan. "We are so far superior in intelligence and morality to all the world, that no others can set us an example in anything." And sadly but naturally enough, this assertion, loudly put forth by some, tacitly inferred by others, is accepted without question by many, because it flatters national or sectional vanity.

To persons of ordinary modesty, or any modesty, the list of names on the other side might well inspire some little hesitation. No distinguished man, except Shelley, ever was a demonstrative and aggressive Aquarian. Will any one have the face to assert that Gough, Dow, Wilson, Greeley, and the other noisy notorieties who march in the van of the Aquarian army, are greater men than Grant and Sherman, Tennyson and Longfellow, Mill and Stanley, Napoleon and Bismarck, and the other remarkable personages of all countries and walks of life who are not Aquarians? I can understand how the fear of being called a drunkard, or friend of drunkenness, should have great influence on a peace-loving individual, in a community making great pretensions to morality; but surely the fear of being considered a conceited idiot, an abettor of obstinate and irrational ignorance, ought to count for something on the other side.

Dismissing, then, this bugbear of imputed wickedness, and estimating the hard names of which the Aquarians are so liberal at their proper value, let us examine the claims of these persons to fasten their sweeping legislation upon us. Ex-Governor Andrew might well say that the Prohibitory laws of Massachusetts were "not strictly consistent with any theory."

We may go further, and assert that the claims of Aquarianism are not logically consistent even before it reaches the Prohibitory stage. But, such as they are, they come under three heads—the Biblical, the Physiological, and the Moral, or more exactly the Moral Police argument. In spite of a good deal of dodging and shifting and manœuvring from one to the other, any plea on their side may be brought under one of these three heads.

The Biblical argument naturally divides itself into investigations of the Old and New Testament. The former we can afford to dispose of briefly. It may be an evidence of great crassitude on my part, but I never could see the reason why learned men should wrangle about *Tirosh*, *Schechar*, and *Gain*, or why the Aquarians, having an impregnable defensive position to fall back on, should go outside of it for the express purpose of stultifying themselves. It is pretty evident that the Jews under their theocracy were permitted a large use of intoxicating liquor. But it is equally true that this only furnishes a *prima facie* evidence in favor of drinking wine, exactly as good, and no better, than the analogous support given by Hebrew practice to slavery and polygamy, two institutions which even the most Judaizing of Puritans have long learned to abhor. The supererogatory work of showing that when the same historians and prophets say *wine* they mean something else, can only have been undertaken by the Aquarians from their natural logical incapacity and irresistible propensity to torture and pervert language. Some instances of this mania on their part are almost incredible. The "American Temperance Society" has lately published, as an authoritative exponent of its views, a book called *Scripture Testimony against Intoxicating Wine*, by the Rev. William Ritchie, (appropriately of) Dunse, Scotland. This treatise breaks ground by affirming, with much parade of reiteration, that because wine is spoken of in different passages of the Old Testament as having different effects, therefore the same thing cannot be meant by the word.* Surely, men who put forth a text-book containing *arguments* like this must have water on the brain.

With the New Testament the case is very different. Of course, the miracle at Cana immediately suggests itself in this connection. It really does seem (I wish to speak with all reverence) as if this miracle was performed and recorded on purpose as a prospective protest and defence against Aquarianism, just as the Parable of the Tares was uttered and recorded as a protest and defence against religious persecution. How do

---

*See the passage quoted at length by D. R. Thomason, *Teetotalism, etc.*, pp. 18 and 99.

the Aquarians get over this testimony? As usual, by a perversion of common sense and ordinary language. They insist that the word οἶνος, which in all recognized Greek authors means an intoxicating liquor, was used by the writers of the New Testament to mean a non-intoxicating liquor,—a piece of reasoning worthy my Lord Peter.*

Indeed, the longer we regard the miracle of Cana, the stronger appears the case. There is more in it than meets the eye. For reasons familiar to the Biblical and historical student, but not necessary to enter upon here, our Saviour and his early disciples practised a more rigid way of life than any large community of moderns has ever professed. They were non-resistants; they held their property in common; some of them abstained from marriage. If, then, we found

---

* "The brother so often mentioned for his erudition, who was well skilled in criticisms, had found in a certain author, which he said should be nameless, that the same word which in the will is called fringe does also signify a broomstick." —*Tale of a Tub*, Section Second.

"Look ye, gentlemen," cries Peter; "to convince you what a couple of blind, positive, ignorant puppies you are, I will use but this plain argument. * * * It [the brown loaf] is as true, good, natural mutton as any in Leadenhall market; and God confound you both eternally if you offer to believe otherwise."—*Ibid.*, Section Fourth.

an explicit record that He or some of His apostles did not use wine, that would be no conclusive argument against its use by us, unless we were also prepared to profess non-resistance, celibacy, and community of goods. But when, on the contrary, our Lord actually went out of his way to make wine, not as a medicine, but for festive purposes, it is wonderful how any man can admit the genuineness and authenticity of St. John's Gospel, and yet call himself an Aquarian from Christian motives.

The Physiological plea of the Aquarians is one of those *soi-disant* arguments which are difficult to hear patiently or answer seriously, so stupendous is the conceit of those who put it forth. In face of the notorious facts that all the most warlike and vigorous races of all times,* the present included, have made a liberal use of fermented liquors; that all athletes use some alcoholic stimulus in training—in fact, can hardly train well without it; that the English upper classes, at this day the most active and powerful body of men in the world, are, to a man (we might almost add, to a woman), large consumers of wine and ale; that our own people, among whom Aquarianism has

---

* Except, possibly, the Saracens. *Possibly*, I say, because it is doubtful how far their practice was consistent with their theory.

gained a considerable foothold, are by no means the healthiest or the longest-lived among nations; that in wine-growing countries the failure of the vintage (as I have myself witnessed in Tuscany) causes an immediate deterioration in the health and appearance of the inhabitants; that the majority of physicians of all schools and countries prescribe the use of wine and beer to numerous classes of patients; in spite of these facts, and many more that might be produced, Aquarians insist that every beverage containing alcohol, even the weakest beer, is a poison, and should only be sold under the same restrictions as other poisons. And why? because some scientific men have instituted experiments to prove, what nobody of common sense ever denied, that raw alcohol is not fit to drink, and that distilled liquors containing a large percentage of alcohol are deleterious to most constitutions, unless used with care and in very moderate quantities. What an insult to human understanding! "Hippocrates may say what he likes, but the coachman is dead." Carpenter and Lallemand may say what they like, but Lord Brougham is alive, and so are many old gentlemen who have used their bodies and minds to some purpose for many years while imbibing this "poison" every day.

The experiments on which Dietarians (not Aquarians merely) rely, are usually of the most extreme character, and as it is attempted to apply them, have absolutely no practical value! You exhibit (as the medical term is) a pinch of snuff to a rabbit; the rabbit sneezes and breaks its neck; therefore tobacco is a deadly poison to man, and its use must be interdicted. You lay a pint of strong green tea on the stomach of a new-born infant; the new-born infant renounces the game of life at the start, and throws up its hand; therefore tea-drinking is a crime only second to the impiety of wine-drinking. You pour a glass of gin down a cat's throat; puss dies in convulsions; therefore lager bier and Bordeaux are not fit to be drunk by human beings. A French *savant* finds a man who is fool enough to swallow a pint of brandy on an empty stomach. The poor wretch unscrews his billiard-table (as the classic slang of the *savant's* metropolis hath it) in thirty-six hours. The only wonder is that he did not die sooner: and we are asked to infer from this experiment that a glass of grog on a cold night is equal to a dose of arsenic and small-pox mixed! *

Putting inferior animals out of the question, conclusions from one individual to others, or to the whole human race, are apt to be among the worst

* The same amount of brandy, properly diluted and administered, at intervals, after a fall or other severe injury, might have been the means of saving the man's life. *Probatum est.*

fallacies of imperfect generalization. A person who should maintain that no man could run a mile in five minutes, because *he* could not run one in ten, would soon be laughed out of court; yet our receptive powers differ quite as much as our active. I consider it very probable that a large glass of raw whiskey would kill me on the spot; at any rate, there is no sum in the Secretary of the Treasury's report that would tempt me to try the experiment; and I am sure that if I were to smoke as many *oscuros* in two days as I have seen General Grant smoke in two hours, a serious, if not fatal illness would be the result. But I have had ocular demonstration that our illustrious warrior can consume this great amount of nicotine without special inconvenience, and I know that there are several men within a stone's throw of me who can imbibe the above amount of Bourbon without serious suffering. In these matters the proverb is emphatically true: "One man's meat is another's poison."

The Aquarians are fond of calling water the natural drink of man. Suppose it could be proved that man, in his natural state, is better without any stimulants, alcoholic or other. What is the practical value of this conclusion? We live in a highly artificial state; not only we, but even the tame animals about us. It is not natural to a horse to wear iron shoes; but it is found very necessary for the work to which we put him. It seems natural to man, in a hot country, to adopt the Diolewisian costume—an umbrella —perhaps not even that.

But in fact the incapacity to use stimulants with benefit is just as likely to be a sign of weakness as of strength. After an unusual physical or mental effort they offer the most efficacious as well as the most pleasant means of recuperation, as any one can testify who has enjoyed either the unpretending lager or the more costly champagne, after a pedestrian excursion, a hard row or ride, or even a *real* college examination. To be sure these are things which the Aquarians rarely understand, for most of them belong to sects which consider athletic sports as rather sinful than otherwise. But the very abuse of stimulants, during the war, showed how the need of them was felt by men whose energies were at work. The human frame was not intended to be a machine so fragile and delicate that it could not deviate occasionally from one particular routine. Thus, it is natural and necessary to pass a part of the twenty-four hours in sleep ; but the man who cannot, under pressure of work or for other good reason, sit up one night without subsequent suffering, is not in the best physical condition—far from it. I think this is a point which ought to be noted, because many persons utter doubting apologies for the use of fermented liquors, only by those who labor under some "vital deficiency;" whereas there are many occasions in which the youngest and strongest and healthiest men may use them with the utmost propriety.

There remains what may be called the moral-police argument, and this must be supposed the strongest, as it influences many who do not insist on the other two. Stripped of the *ad captandum* Billingsgate which is its usual accompaniment, it runs somehow thus :

Intemperance is a great vice and a great evil. It causes numerous breaches of the peace, and other offences and crimes, including murders. Ten per cent. (in round numbers) of the national mortality may be charged to its account. It is a more fruitful source of insanity than even camp-meetings and religious revivals. It disables many men from supporting their wives and children, who thus become a public burden and increase the taxes. (This is usually presented by and to the New England mind as. the climax.) For more than forty years good men have been preaching and exhorting against it ; yet it still flourishes. As the grass of moral suasion has not been sufficiently effectual, we must try the stones of prohibitory legislation. If men can find no ardent spirits to drink, of course they will not get drunk. Let us, therefore, prohibit the manufacture, transportation, and sale of distilled liquors. But to do this effectually, it is also necessary to prohibit the manufacture, transportation, and sale of fermented liquors, because one man's temperate use of wine or beer is made an excuse for another man's intemperate use of rum or whiskey.* True, this is a great invasion of personal liberty; but we have incurred so many taxes for liberty, that we cannot afford to pay any more, especially as we need any possible surplus to "protect" home industry. Nor can the persons thus debarred from their usual beverages justly complain, if we can only get a popular vote in favor of our measure, for this is a government of the majority. The majority can do no wrong; the minority have no right, except that of grumbling. Neither can they pretend (except in some peculiar cases) that drinking fermented liquors is necessary for their life: it is only subservient to their comfort and pleasure. That comfort and pleasure they ought to be willing to give up for the sake of the public morality and economy, consoling themselves with the reflection that they are indirectly contributing to diminish the percentage of mortality and lower the taxes.

I have tried to state the argument fairly; indeed,

---

* Similarly, if A wishes to marry, and B does not, because he thinks he cannot afford it, A's marriage should be forbidden, lest it be made an excuse for B's fornication.

the effort to do so has cost me more time and trouble than any other two pages in the book. Yet, sometimes it has been too much for me. The Aquarian arguments are so incoherent and fallacious that the mere attempt to enunciate one of them, in a regular and connected form, is generally enough to show its absurdity to any one who has a habit of close reasoning. Doing our best to detect a coherent nucleus, we succeed in evolving these two propositions :

First, that the abuse of anything is a conclusive reason for suppressing all similar or analogous things; wherefore, secondly, because a great vice exists, it is our duty to put down, at whatever cost, everything in the remotest degree connected with or ancillary to it.

The results of these principles we shall see more clearly by applying them to other prevalent vices.

And the first which I shall take up for the purpose of illustration and comparison is prostitution, which *unreasoners*, like Greeley, are accustomed to call the violation of the Seventh Commandment. Of course, it is nothing of the sort—the Seventh Commandment having reference to a special variety of illicit intercourse, with a special independent element. (This is a small matter, but worth noticing as an exemplification of the confusion of mind under which men like Greeley labor, and which hinders them from express-

4*

ing the simplest proposition correctly.) That prostitution is a vice of tremendous extent and influence, every one admits, and it would generally be recognized as more essentially vicious in its character than intemperance, which many regard only as an abuse. Thus, none but the most rabid Aquarians consider the mere act of drinking a glass of light wine or beer as a sin in itself, apart from the example; but all Christians agree that the act of fornication is wrong in itself.* Even among Europeans of Latin descent, who commonly wink at the practice, it is theoretically condemned, and no person professing to be specially devout, could openly indulge in it without subjecting himself to censure. But setting all this aside as an unnecessary refinement of speculation, and confining

* When we reflect that venereal disease was almost entirely unknown to the ancients, and is generally unknown to savages before their acquaintance with civilized men, persons who still believe in the moral government of the world may be pardoned for supposing (*pace* the memory of Mr. Buckle) that chastity is a virtue peculiar to the Christian religion, and the *new* virtue which it introduced. Of course, it would not follow from this, as the sage Greeley supposes, that it is wrong to protect, by legislative action or medical skill, the sinner from the physical consequences of his transgression, any more than it is right to oppress the Jew or the negro—both which practices have been defended on like scriptural and historical grounds.

ourselves to intemperance, in the true sense of the word, acknowledged by all to be an evil, when we compare it with licentiousness, we see that the latter is as efficient a servant of sin as the former, from whatever point of view we contemplate its ravages. It destroys the peace of families. It gives rise to numerous crimes—to embezzlements and robberies, to broils and murders. It is the cause of diseases and insanities, premature deaths and deterioration of the species. It demoralizes the community and increases the number of pensioners on the public. Surely here, if anywhere, is a subject for Prohibitive legislation, pursuing the evil to its very roots.

I have no doubt that many very well-intentioned persons consider it quite possible to do so, and wonder why it has not yet been done. It is not easy for the inhabitants of a country town or village to understand the difficulties, moral and political, of dealing with men in great masses. Nor does this assertion cast any slur upon the wisdom or intelligence of the country-dwellers within their proper sphere. It only states a simple fact, that they have not experience of other phases of society. The difference of the means available in a small and large community is continually making itself manifest in a variety of ways. A lady who had long conducted with much success a small and select female school in a New England village, made public her experience some years ago for the benefit of her pupils, some of whom had adopted her own vocation. Among her bits of advice was this : "Never appeal to emulation by giving prizes or rewards." And doubtless she, in her little family (for such the school was), had never felt the necessity of invoking the spirit of emulation ; but a great majority of those connected with any large academical institution of boys or young men could bear testimony to its potency and necessity in such places.

So, too, it is quite possible that in a village or country town, where the people have been from the first properly educated in this respect, a satisfactory standard of purity may be attained, and that, too, without much special legislation. In one of these hamlets where, as a friend of mine once said, "you can't kiss a woman without alarming the neighborhood," we may satisfy all the material requisitions of technical morality, especially since a small community can always protect itself by expelling its unworthy members. But the moment you apply this regimen to a large town or city, innumerable difficulties present themselves. In the first place, the most annoying violations of personal liberty would be necessary. It would be requisite to arrest every female found alone in the streets after dark, as she *might* be a "social evil." It would be incumbent on every couple stopping at a hotel to prove their identity and exhibit their marriage certificate. Every house suspected—not of being disorderly or a nuisance, any such limitation the theory of Prohibition despises—but of containing vicious people, must be turned inside out forthwith.

Next, everything which may possibly become, or may be supposed capable of becoming, accessory to prostitution must be suppressed without mercy. The theatres, whether running in their own name or under the *aliases* of museums, lecture-rooms, academies, etc., must be closed; for have not grave divines denounced the theatre as a nursery to the brothel? With the theatre must go the opera; for is it not written in the books of Titcomb that the opera hath "licentious revelations?" All "promiscuous" dancing (as it is called in the elegant vocabulary of the sectarian press) must be put down by force of law, because some fashionable dances are of doubtful propriety. A very extensive raid must be made upon literature; one which, starting with Swinburne and Walt Whitman, would not altogether spare Tennyson, and might be expected to end in a general expurgation of everybody. Lastly, the length of women's dresses in both directions must be regulated by law, for there are those whose delicate virtue cannot behold without emotion an ankle or a shoulder of the other gender.

Here is Prohibition applied to the "social evil." Well, suppose it has all been carried out according to the most sanguine anticipations of the reformers, and that prostitution is suppressed. What then? I am very much afraid that human frailty would find another vent, and that we should have a largely increased violation of the Seventh Commandment as the very first result of our reform. In short, that we should substitute not merely one vice for another, but, all things considered, a greater for a less.* To be sure, this result is only hypothetical, for we have never had the Prohibitory system carried out in this direction; but it is by far the most probable one to any man with a reasonable knowledge of history and human nature.

Now let us go back to our Aquarian Prohibition. We see in this case analogous violations of personal liberty carried out. We see everything that can tend, however indirectly, to intemperance, crushed down. We see every person, not merely who is a temperate user of the "wine that maketh glad the heart of man," but who hesitates to join the Aquarians in their

---

* Strictly speaking, it would be the substitution of a crime for a vice; but this is not important to the illustration.

crusade against non-Aquarians, abused and slandered, vilified and calumniated. It really looks as if these persecuting meddlers would eventually succeed in prohibiting the use of fermented beverages throughout the whole country. What would be the consequence? There are symptoms already which enable us to guess.

First, it is obvious that the consumption of tobacco would be enormously increased. Every man who is in the habit of using both alcoholic beverages and tobacco, when, from any cause short of complete prostration by sickness, he is temporarily deprived of the former indulgence, has a propensity to "take it out" in the latter. Those men who, without any parade of superior virtue, have renounced wine for sanitary or other reasons, are apt to be great smokers. The observation of individual cases justifies us in assuming that were the consumption of fermented and distilled liquors to cease, that of tobacco would be increased, as I have phrased it, *enormously*. And I hardly think that any man, however fond of the weed, or impervious to its bad effects, can say that this is a result greatly to be desired. I do not hesitate to lay down this proposition, fully convinced that a large majority of medical men in all countries would bear me out: If the consumption of wine, beer, and spirits, in our own or any other country, were to cease entirely, and that of tobacco to increase proportionately, *the physical condition of the people would not be improved.* I think, indeed, we ought to go further, and say that their morals and manners would not be greatly improved, though there might well be a diminution in the number of crimes against the person. Tobacco, unless used in great moderation, or by persons of very powerful constitutions, weakens and injures men in many ways. It upsets the stomachs of some and the nerves of others ; and where any disorder of the heart exists, is more mischievous than any fermented liquor can be. Its harmful effects on certain constitutions take a wide range, from petty annoyances, like blisters on the lips, to the most serious afflictions, such as weakening of the intellect. If using anything which can cause intoxication be the one unpardonable sin, consumers of tobacco are certainly involved in it, for tobacco frequently intoxicates. To be sure, this drunkenness being only narcotic, and not preceded nor followed by exhilaration, does not, like the drunkenness of alcohol, incite to breaches of the peace ; but then, on the other hand, the most moderate use of it in public is a great annoyance to those who do not like it, in which respect it is the most selfish of luxuries. And if it be a strong argument, as Aquarians affirm, against the use of beverages containing alcohol, that the taste for them grows upon the consumer, this applies with double and more than double force to tobacco, as the experience of every man who has himself used both articles, and is conversant with the habits of their users, can testify. In fine, almost every charge against fermented drinks is also applicable to tobacco; wherefore, the most consistent Aquarians already openly maintain that, as soon as they have succeeded in putting down the former, they will suppress the latter.

Well, let us suppose tobacco also prohibited, and the smoker, like the drinker, lurking in holes and corners, or fled to some comparatively free country. Still, somehow or other, people *will* have narcotic stimulants. The whole community will not be deprived of them. As you drive out wine and tobacco on one side, opium and hachish slip in on the other. One effect of the Aquarian agitation has already been to double the consumption of opium in the United States, notwithstanding the great increase in its price. Let Aquarianism go on, and in twenty or thirty years we may be a people of opium-smokers, and speculative foreigners will debate whether this terrible vice was introduced by the Chinese through California, or grew solely out of Prohibitive legislation.*

---

* We need not dwell on the mischiefs likely to arise

In using the illustration and making the comparison which I have just done, it is quite possible that some may tax me with indelicacy and irrelevancy.

In respect of the former charge, I can only shelter myself under the example of an eminent English judge (the late Baron Alderson), whom I once heard repeating some gross expressions of a witness. There was a titter in the court. "Gentlemen," said he to the jury, "there is no indecency in a court of justice." What they wanted was to get at the truth; and decorum must not be allowed to stand in the way of that result. When our liberties are so seriously threatened by the Interferists, it is necessary to show the extent of the danger, even if, in order to do so, we must trample on a few conventionalities.

As to the latter, it is a very common, because very convenient one. The easiest way to get rid of an inconvenient chain of reasoning, is to say that the reasoner sets up "men of straw." *It is an objection of which we cannot be too suspicious.* Very often it proceeds from the objector's ignorance of what has been

---

from a largely increased consumption of tea and coffee, because, though in our exciting climate such increased use would be very injurious, it could not strictly come under the head of vice. But it is worth noticing, in this connection, that the vegetarians and all the sternest Aquarians proscribe tea and coffee.

said on the topic under discussion ; very often, also, from his incapacity to draw inferences and follow principles to their results.

In fact, the natural relations of the sexes are one of the first things that an interfering ruler or moralist is apt to lay hold of. Their legitimate connection, in a certain sense the creature of law, has been a fruitful subject of legal experiments, and real or fancied philosophers have in most cases labored rather to tighten than to lighten existing fetters. From Plato, who destroyed the family tie for the most important class in his imaginary "Republic" (not for the whole of that Republic, as the learned Greeley once asserted), down, in every sense, to the Kentucky Legislature—who having discovered, the other day, that there was an extra percentage of idiocy among the issue of first cousins (it does not appear how many of the Legislature were the result of such unions), forthwith recommended that the marriage of first cousins should be prohibited—the constant tendency has been to multiply restrictions. As to the illicit relations of the sexes—but there is no use of going into a historical disquisition about them, when our case lies just at hand. Of the probable results of Prohibitive legislation, which I have enumerated, *the greater part have been actually proposed.* Dancing has always been under the Puritan ban. Theatrical amusements have been, possibly are still, illegal in some parts of New England. The propositions most verging on the grotesque, such as the suppression of poets and novelists, and the legal regulation of out-door female dress, I have myself, within a few months, seen advocated in very respectable and non-sectarian papers. The danger, then, is no imaginary one, though most of these reforms are still in the ante-Prohibition stage.

Let us now look at Prohibition as applicable to another vice. No one, I presume, will deny that gambling is one of the great moral curses of our country. It may be more prevalent in the West than in the East—in great cities than in small villages; but, on the whole, it is sufficiently common to be justly entitled a national vice. Nor is it necessary to expatiate on the terrible evils of which it is the cause—the distress and ruin of families, the forgeries and defalcations, the murders and suicides. Surely, this mighty sin should be attacked. Well, then, let us attack it on Prohibition principles.

What has Government done to suppress gambling? Nothing. What ought it to do? Everything.

Our legislative enactments on the subject vary in different States, but, briefly, they amount to this: Gambling debts (wages included) are not recoverable by law; public gaming houses are forbidden (at least in all settled parts of our country), and "hells," *nominally* private, are *occasionally* molested by the police.* Behold what *is* done. Now, what should be our Prohibition principles? We must prohibit the manufacture and sale of all possible implements of gambling—cards, dice, etc., for though they may be, and often are, used innocently, they are always capable of guilty use. We must shut up all public billiard-rooms, for publicly-played games of billiards give rise to betting, and, though betting and gambling are by no means the same thing, yet there is a certain analogy and connection between them, and the former has a much greater tendency to slide into the latter than the drinking of beer into the drinking of whiskey. The turf, in all its branches, must be put down—not for the Puritan reason, "because it gives pleasure to the spectators," but because races are made an occasion of betting. Nay, we must prohibit all very fast horses, of whatever gait; for, though a man may re-

---

* The italics are used with a purpose. Probably there are twenty hells in full blast every night in any half mile of Broadway, between Canal-street and Madison-Square. At the fashionable watering-places these establishments are so well known that even non-gamblers frequent them; for instance, gentlemen starving at the Newport hotels, go there to get supper. I mention these things because some innocent country gentlemen, who write in the newspapers, appear to think the laws do not permit gambling.

fuse to trot his "flyers" for money, people will be sure to bet on their performances whenever they are exhibited in public. So Bonner must be suppressed; Beecher can't save him. Base-ball, and cricket, and regattas must go the same way, for all these are bet-on-able. Finally, let every man who has ever attended a horse-race, or bet a pair of gloves, be denounced as a gambler, or friend of gambling. No, not finally. Thus far all chimes in excellently with the Puritan idea, which denounces all these amusements as sinful. But can we consistently stop at amusements? There is no end of downright gambling in Wall-street and other commercial centres—gambling (thinly disguised under the name of speculation) in stocks, in flour, in cotton, in gold. All this traffic, therefore, must be put under Government supervision, and the absurd gold-bill of Thaddeus Stevens, at once the laughing-stock and the terror of the mercantile world, must be adopted as a pattern of legislation. What a nice specimen of a free government we should have! What a glorious specimen of a model republic!* Yet this is the legitimate and natural result of Prohibition.

---

* In fact, freedom is the least thing these people care about. What they want is *the right to oppress and worry* others. An Aquarian agent recently told me that he considered Hell the only free government.

There is one more illustration, about the production of which I somewhat hesitate, for the vice which supplies it is not generally recognized as a vice—at least in practice—by Puritans and Prohibitionists. They do not remember, or do not choose to remember, that "whatsoever goeth out of the mouth defileth a man." Falsehood in a good cause—*i. e.*, their own—they consider, if not like the Jesuits an actual virtue, at any rate a slight and pardonable offence. Nevertheless, I believe that most Protestant Christians will bear me out in considering falsehood, calumny, and slander as very vicious and sinful; and it is evident to any man, Christian or not, that they are frequently productive of great harm. Especially is this the case when they are circulated in print among hundreds of thousands of readers. The *Herald*, in its early days, drove some weak-minded individuals to suicide; and though this could hardly happen again now, since the very virulence of the evil has partly wrought its own cure, and newspaper statements about individuals meet comparatively little credence, still the general tendency to debauch the public mind, by accustoming it to falsehood, remains in full force. According to Prohibition principles, it is evident that in order to put a speedy check to this practice, a censorship of the press is necessary. It must be a general and universal censorship, for though many papers are now decent and truthful, they may be tempted some day to follow the example of the *Herald* and *Tribune,* just as the moderate drinker *may* become a drunkard.

This investigation might easily be extended. Some writers have carried it further, and inferred very plausibly that Prohibition eventuates in Socialism and abolition of private property; but I think enough has been said to show that the moral-police principle generally carried out would produce an arbitrary government of the most irritating and intolerable kind. Imperial France or Austria would be a very free country in comparison with America under a pure Prohibitionist *régime.*

"But," says the Aquarian, "shall this great evil of intemperance be rampant in the land, and shall I not essay to abate it?" Certainly; by all truly moral means—by your example and your influence. Every earnest Christian man will have a higher moral standard than the people about him—by *people,* I mean *both* the mass of the community and his own peculiar set. But this is his own standard, which he has no right to force upon others. Just consider how many topics of life there are, major and minor, on which men's ideas of right and propriety differ. How can one individual give law to another in these things? If I think certain dances indecent, I may abstain from them, and refuse to have them taught to my children ; but I have no right to make or try to make the perpetration of the polka a penitentiary offence. If I believe that some or all theatrical representations are immoral, no one obliges me to witness them : why should I seek to deprive of their amusement my neighbors, who (possibly after quite as careful an examination of the subject) have arrived at a different conclusion ? If I consider the *Herald* and the *Tribune* huge agents of public corruption, I do not buy them or suffer them to enter my house ; but I cannot prevent others from purchasing them. If I imagine that servants' liveries are hostile to Republican government (there are some grown men who really believe this, and hold that the presence of a few dozen breeches-wearing Irish and negro grooms in a public park threatens to subvert our institutions), I have a full and perfect right to let my coachman dress himself like an omnibus driver, a scarecrow, or a Methodist parson, as he pleases ; but I have no business to pull Mr. Belmont's tiger out of his boots. The old law-maxim, *Sic utere tuo ut non alienam lædas*, is a very good rule in most such cases. For instance, if a band of rowdies disturb a quiet congregation by their outcries, or annoy people going to church, there is good reason why the law should take hold of them ; but if you see a man driving out into the country on

Sunday afternoon, it is not a valid plea for forcibly interfering with him that he shocks your moral sense by what you call violating the Sabbath. If a drinking hole is a centre of crime and riot, its keeper "injures others' property" too much to be allowed to "use his own" in that way; but when a knot of orderly Germans are quaffing their beer in a garden, you have no moral or equitable grounds for turning them out because you hold a theory that every fluid containing a drop of alcohol is poison, or that οἶνος in the New Testament means something different from what it does in all other Greek books. Nay, there are cases in which the maxim must be a little loosely construed in favor of individual liberty. There are ways in which a man may indirectly inflict pecuniary injury on me, without my being able to prevent or punish him. One wealthy man in a small community may, through ostentation, or carelessness, or faulty good-nature, raise the standard of prices for his less wealthy neighbors. Unless they can, by friendly expostulation, prevail on him to change his way of life, it is hard to say what remedy they can or ought to have. I have known one landlord, by letting his house too low, throw down the rents of a whole neighborhood. The other proprietors suffered; but he surely had a right to do what he did. And the reason of such exceptions is not difficult to trace. We cannot right the small wrong without committing a greater, or reach the equity of the particular instance without violating broad general principles.

The greater number of such matters in every-day life are regulated by common sense, that most ordinary form of common sense which tells a man that he should not go from Boston to New York by way of China, or "turn in" to bed with his hat on; that he should not ask his doctor to mend his boots, or call in the constable when his wife is to be delivered, or turn to the *Tribune* when he wants to know the truth of any matter. Now, Deacon Coldstream, can't you apply a little of this ordinary common sense to your dealings with other men on the subject of what you call temperance? You drink water; I don't wish to prevent you from doing so. I don't think any the worse of you for doing so. Indeed, I don't think about it at all. You are supposed to be old enough to know what is good for you; and if you are not, it is none of my business. If you believe that all fermented beverages are poisonous, of course you do right not to touch them. I, who have arrived at a different conclusion, claim to enjoy an equal liberty. Why not let me have it? It will be better for both of us, and for charity and good feeling generally. As long as you do not try to "prohibit" me, you are only an extraordinary moral phenomenon, to be contemplated from a distance without apprehension, and even with some degree of mild curiosity; but when you strike at my travelling comforts, or actually threaten to invade my house and "dash from my lips" what you are pleased to miscall "the wine-cup," you become a social pestilence and a personal enemy.

You believe in free institutions—at least you think you do. You also hold that a people should be moral in the largest sense of the term. So much ground have we in common. Do you seriously hope to advance either freedom or morality by Prohibition? Freedom you certainly will not. The very examples of generally approved Prohibition show in the strongest light its incompatibility with freedom. It has been found necessary to prohibit the use of alcoholic drinks by the rank and file of the army at certain times. It has been found expedient to prohibit their use by students in certain cases. But neither soldiers nor students are under free government. They are subject to laws more or less arbitrary, which they had no share in making.

On morality the good effect of your Prohibition is more apparent than real. There is a forced external conformity, dearly paid for by the drawbacks enumerated in the preceding chapter. It is by indirectly working with moral means that real moral reforms are effected. You may see one conspicuous instance of this among ourselves. Despite all our self-congratulation about republican virtue, the candid and well-informed observer will confess that we are less truthful than some nations, less honest than several, less temperate than many. But in one respect—namely, in what concerns domestic morality—however short of an ideal standard, we take comparatively a very high place, perhaps the highest. Now, whatever be the cause of this superiority, it certainly is not Prohibition nor Draconian legislation. Our laws against adultery and seduction are not more severe than those of most civilized countries. Our marriage-tie, is, if anything, rather looser. There is no censorship of the press in the interest of domestic virtue; but there is a healthier public opinion on the subject. Why not trust to a like influence in behalf of temperance, real temperance? Why, by your unwarrantable interference with private liberty and comfort, infuse into the discussion of important and delicate moral questions the same bitterness which so long rendered the very name of religion odious, and still too often makes the mere mention of party politics a nuisance.

CONCLUSION.

PRETTY much every theoretical principle is subject to practical exceptions; it is precisely in these that the difficulty of its practical application consists. I suspect that most readers of Mill's remarkable work on "Liberty" have felt his conclusions to be somewhat of a falling-off. At the same time, I do not see why a writer, who is not a lawgiver nor law-maker, should be forced to explain and adjust every possible application of his general rule, especially when that rule is essentially negative. We say, "Hands off! No 'paternal' interference with personal liberty; no Protection, no Prohibition!" If you ask, "But may not Protection be temporarily beneficial under certain circumstances? May not the chance of suppressing or abating a particular vice authorize an infringement on private freedom?" I answer: The particular case must be decided according to its own circumstances, always bearing in mind these two things: First, that the burden of proof always rests on the opponents of freedom. Secondly, that unless you can be very sure of your result beforehand, you are incurring a certain evil for an uncertain good. Liberty is too precious a commodity to be experimented with, *à la* Greeley, for the mere sake of experimenting.

Nevertheless, I am willing, in a broad and general way, to enter into some particulars, for the purpose of contrasting the two systems in their application.

Education is granted by most persons to be a necessary support of free institutions. But all parents will not send their children to school, even when they can do so without payment. Such being the case, the legislator may attack the evil in two ways. He may make a law compelling all children of the requisite physical ability, between certain ages, to attend school for a certain period of the year, regardless of their circumstances and wishes and those of their parents. He will thus secure an appearance of uniform education—I say appearance, because bringing a horse (or a donkey) to the well of knowledge does not involve his drinking : this he will do at the expense of a decided violation of the parents' right. Or, on the other hand, he may say, We oblige no man to be educated or to educate his children ; but no man utterly uneducated is fit for a republican citizen ; therefore no man shall vote unless he can read and write. We do not prescribe the time at which or the way in which the man is to be educated; but we make a certain amount of education a *sine qua non* for suffrage.

(This is an extreme case, and purposely chosen as such. Most of the stoutest "Liberty" men, including Mill himself, allow, nay, insist on the State's right to educate all members of the community, whether they choose or not. But I believe that the general principle need not be violated in this particular case, and that the way which I have pointed out secures at once public interests and private rights.

It is desirable to encourage native industry. On that point we are all agreed. But there are two very different ways of doing or attempting to do so. Government may put on a duty here and a bounty there, bolstering up special interests, one after another, as they have strength and pertinacity to urge their claims. The natural end of this is, that everybody clamorous enough is more or less "protected," which is very like trying to win at roulette by putting money on all the numbers. Or, it may exert itself to remove, as far as possible, all fetters from commerce, thus indirectly assisting the people to economize their industry by producing those articles for the production of which their country is best fitted, so that they will obtain the greatest possible reward for their labor.

A certain vice is alarmingly prevalent, and requires to be checked. There are two ways of operating against it. You may endeavor by the most stringent enactments to stamp out everything which can, by the most ingenious exaggeration and misconstruction, be possibly made out ancillary to it—no matter how flagrant your interference with personal liberty and comfort—no matter how much odium you may excite against law and lawgivers generally—no matter how much deception you encourage in the people—no matter how much falsehood you are forced to promulgate yourselves—no matter how many new vices you may cause to spring up before you have succeeded in crushing out the old one. Or, refusing to infer vice where it does not exist, and to punish one man in advance for the possible fault of another, you may attack the enemy indirectly, forwarding all vehicles of moral and intellectual improvement, and at the same time promoting, by all available means, the physical improvement of the masses,—one way of doing which is, not to discourage, but, on the contrary, encourage all proper amusements, especially out-door recreations.*

Other illustrations might be adduced, but the above are sufficient. The principle is always the same:

---

* Even merely Epicurean considerations may be conducive to morality. Thus, it has frequently been observed that bad cookery promotes intemperance, and good cookery diminishes it.

on the one hand, liberty, respect for the rights of the individual, limited only by the similar individual rights of those with whom he comes in contact ; on the other, a petty tyranny of perpetual government interference with daily pursuits, a tyranny none the less such because imposed by a majority instead of an autocrat or an aristocracy. Indeed, the tyranny may well be more oppressive in the former case than in the latter ; for an autocrat or an aristocracy, after taking the best of everything for themselves, will make some provision for the rest out of the rest, while a popular majority knows only what *it* wants, and cannot appreciate the condition of its opponents. When the Protective-Prohibition-Paternal theory shall have been carried out according to the wishes and designs of its advocates, when every man's food, and drink, and locomotion shall be regulated by law, and all his clothes and tools cost twice as much as they ought to, what becomes of that liberty for which we have renounced so many of the ornaments and accomplishments, the decencies and refinements of European civilization, for which we have just spent hundreds of thousands of lives and thousands of millions of money ?

Will you say that a man's religious freedom is untouched, his liberty of conscience unfettered, that he is free to worship God as he likes ? This is but the result of a lucky accident: in the multiplicity of sects no one has yet been able to gain a complete local predominance. This may not always be the case, and the probable consequences of a change may be seen in what has already resulted from the incomplete predominance of the Romanists in the city of New York. They have compelled the Protestants to pay taxes to and for them, they have blocked up the streets with their processions and the squares with their bazaars.

Will you say that he has the ballot? So has the French peasant. France stands before us, a Providential warning how easily universal suffrage may co-exist with other institutions the reverse of free.

But, you say, he has freedom of speech; he can declaim, and write, and publish what he pleases. Well, to be sure it is something to be able *liberare animam suam.* It is some small comfort to be allowed openly to call a Greeley a Greeley. But it is only a small comfort after all. In the daily life of ordinary men, doing is more important than saying. If you are shut up in prison, it does not help you much to curse your jailer. You would rather make him a polite bow outside the wall. Besides, it is not always easy or even possible for un unpopular person or cause to get a hearing. Editors do not care to print what is unpopular; nor can we blame them much for this, since writing is a business like any other, and men cannot go on with it unless they make money by it. The same may be said, up to a certain point, and with a few exceptions, of publishers. As to publishing unpopular ideas at one's own expense, it is a luxury which none but a millionaire can allow himself frequently.

Yet, feeble and inefficient as this protection is, it is the best we have, and we must make the best of it, and trust to reaching, by its means, Anglo-Saxon common sense and Anglo-Saxon sensitiveness to attacks on personal freedom,—qualities which, however occasionally obscured, are permanent and valuable traits of our great race. I send out this little book with a very faint hope that it may make some Interferist reflect, and pause in his design of lording it over his neighbors' concerns and habits, and forcing every one to live according to his moral and social standard. I send it out with somewhat more expectation, that it may here and there stir up some right-minded and liberal, but too easy man, to the necessity of taking a bold stand in defence of his rights. For the peril is imminent and formidable. While making huge strides forward in one direction, we have slipped back without knowing it nearly as far in another. Well did the great Hungarian orator say, that God has bestowed two supreme boons on man—

celestial bliss hereafter, and liberty on earth. Under a delusive pretence of helping us to the first, the fanatical votaries of Interference would deprive us of the second.

LAKESIDE, LENOX, MASS.,
August 15, 1867.

Spooner's Biographical History of the

Fine Arts, being Memoirs of the Lives and Works of Eminent Painters, Engravers, Sculptors and Architects, from the earliest ages to the present time. Alphabetically arranged and condensed from the best authorities; including the works of Vasari, Lanzi, Kugler, Dr. Waagen, Bryan, Pilkington, Walpole, Sir C. Eastlake, and Mrs. Jameson. With Chronological Tables of Artists and their Schools, Plates of Monograms, &c. Fourth Edition. 2 vols., Royal Octavo. Cloth, $10.00. Half Morocco, $15.00.

"The most complete and desirable Cyclopædia of Art-Biography extant. Artists and Connoisseurs should as soon think of being without Webster's Dictionary, as a copy of this edition of Spooner."—*N. Y. Tribune.*

"The Supplement, the copious collection of monograms and artists' devices, and the introductory review on painting, give this edition of Spooner's Dictionary the advantage over every other Cyclopædia of Art-Biography now extant."—*N. Y. Times.*

"Quite an event in the art-world."—*N. Y. Evening Post.*

"In many respects superior to Bryan, even in his last editions."—*Journal of Commerce.*

"We are astonished by the magnitude and result of the labor here expended. It is the work which thousands of non-professional men have desired to possess."—*N. Y. Observer.*

"A work indispensable to all who love, study, or cultivate Art, and brought out with a view equally to beauty and economy."—*Boston Transcript.*

Critical and Social Essays. Reprinted

from the New York Nation. 12mo. Cloth, $1.50.

"The combination of literary and political discussions of so uncommon excellence, free from vulgarity and flippancy, may almost be said to mark an epoch in American Journalism."—*New Englander.*

"All are entertaining, clever, and well-written; and some of them deserve the higher praise of being the condensed statement of vigorous thought upon questions of practical importance. The value of these essays is not purely literary, but consists much more in the reflection they afford of the best thinking and temper of the times in their sympathetic and intelligent criticisms of prevailing forms of life. We trust that this is but the first of a series of similar volumes."—*North American Review.*

"They are an honor to American Journalism."—*N. Y. Citizen.*

"In fine, we like all these articles from the *Nation*, for the reasons that we like the *Nation*, which has been, in a degree singular among newspapers, conscientious and candid in literary matters; while in affairs of social and political interest, it has shown itself friendly to everything that could advance civilization, and notably indifferent to the claims of persons and parties."—*Atlantic Monthly.*

Thackeray's Works. A Uniform Edition.

16mo., gilt top, claret-colored morocco cloth. $1.25 per vol. Half mor. $2.00 per vol.

Vanity Fair	3 vols.
Pendennis	3 "
Henry Esmond	2 "
The English Humorists	1 "
The Newcomes	4 "
The Virginians	4 "
The Four Georges; Lovel the Widower	1 "
Adventures of Philip	2 "
The Great Hoggarty Diamond; Book of Snobs	1 "
The Kickleburys Abroad; Rebecca and Rowena, &c.	1 "
Major Gahagan; Fatal Boots; Ballads.	1 "
Yellowplush Papers	1 "
Sketches, Novels by Eminent Hands	1 "
Memoirs of Barry Lyndon	1 "
The Fitz Boodle Papers; a Shabby Genteel Story, &c.	1 "
Men's Wives	1 "
Denis Duval	1 "

Each work sold separately.

Charles Kingsley's Works. 16 mo.

(uniform with Thackeray). Oak-colored cloth, gilt top, $1.25 per vol. Half mor. $2.00 per vol.

Yeast	1 vol.
Westward Ho!	2 "
Two Years Ago	2 "
Hypatia	2 "
Alton Locke	1 "
Hereward the Wake	2 "

Each work sold separately.

Beethoven's Letters, 1790-1826. From the collection of Dr. L. Nohl. Translated by Lady Wallace. With a portrait and facsimile. 2 vols., 12mo. Cloth, gilt top. $3.50.

In this collection of his private correspondence we have an interior view of the great composer—showing us what he was, what he did, what he suffered, and what was the point of view from which he surveyed art and life. Beethoven, in music, is quite as great a name as Milton's in poetry; and among the thousands who have been charmed, thrilled and exalted by his wonderful melodies, and who really appreciate the originality, creativeness and might of his genius, these letters cannot fail to find delighted readers.—*Boston Transcript.*

Mozart's Letters, 1769-1791. Translated, from the collection of L. Nohl, by Lady Wallace. 2 vols., 12mo. With a portrait and facsimile. Cloth, gilt top. $3.50.

These letters have the charm of Mozart's loving melodies. They are not less gay and tender, not less tremulous with sensibility, and seem to let us into the secret of his felicitous ease in composition—the secret of a bird "Singing of summer with full-throated Ease.—*G. H. Lewes, in Fortnightly Review.*

Delightful volumes of the letters of Wolfgang Amadeus Mozart, the composer, that, like his music, are warm and bright, bespeaking the genial and loving spirit that has ever made Mozart a favorite. It is through a man's private letters, designed simply for the eye of affection, that we ascertain the true character. We seem to sit with him and hear his voice in generous bursts of musical fervor, or in social love, or in friendly regard and inquiry, experiencing a pleasure different, but still as great, as that we experience when listening to his grand compositions—*Boston Saturday Evening Gazette.*

The Art Principle and its Application to the Teaching of Music. By Anna Jackson. 16 mo., Cloth. Price, 40 cents.

"The pamphlet ought to be in the hands of every teacher and every father whose children receive music-lessons."—*Musical Review.*

Abrégé de l'Histoire de l'Art. Par Dr. E. Förster 16mo. 60 cents.

The Same, in German. 16mo. 60 cents.

Excellent little sketch of the history of fine arts from the earliest time to the present.

www.ingramcontent.com/pod-product-compliance
Lightning Source LLC
LaVergne TN
LVHW021426110826
845150LV00007B/2097

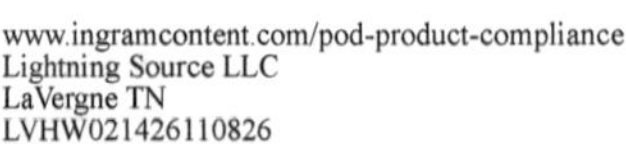

* 9 7 8 1 4 2 5 5 0 8 4 7 0 *